How to Make $$$

Buying and Selling

Small Businesses

A Turnaround Manual

■

By Ernie Stech,
Business Consultant

A Business Book
from
Chief Mountain Publishing

This publication is designed to provide accurate and authoritative information in regard to the subject matter covered. It is sold with the understanding that the publisher is not engaged in rendering legal, accounting, or other professional service. If legal advice or other expert opinion is required, the service of a competent professional person should be sought. From a Declaration of Principle jointly adopted by a Committee of the American Bar Association and a Committee of Publishers.

Publisher's Cataloging in Publication
(Prepared by Quality Books, Inc.)

Stech, Ernest L., 1933-
    How to make $$$ buying and selling small businesses: a turnaround manual / Ernie Stech. --1st ed.
    p. cm.
    Includes bibliographical references and index.
    ISBN 0-9645661-4-1

1. Sale of small businesses. 2. Small business–Purchasing.
3. Investments. I. Title.

HD1393.25.S84 1996   658.1'6
                                   QB196-20201

"Ernie showed me how to make a lot more money with my small business than I ever imagined possible."

— *Vicki Thomas, President, Documents On Demand, Inc.*

"If your fear of overwork, boring tasks, or dead-end products is stopping you from buying a business, Ernie's thorough guide is the refreshing approach you need. Intending to buy, upgrade... the process allows you to innovate and work in a variety of industries and with different people."

— *Margaret Nielsen, Founder ToyBox Storage Systems*

"The thirty-plus years of Ernie's small business ownership, management, and consulting comes through in this book. It is well worth reading for anyone thinking about buying a business."

— *Richard H. Frost, Chairman Emeritus, Frost Engineering Development Corp.*

Table of Contents

Acknowledgments

My deepest appreciation to Barbara Rice and Rebecca Taylor for their dedicated efforts to correct my editorial and typographic errors. I also need to thank the hundreds of person who have attended seminars and workshops on how to buy small businesses and who provided me with new insights and valuable information.

Chapter 1

THE PROCESS

Buy low; sell high. That's the traditional advice given to all investors. And that's what we all try to do. In the stock market, it takes some real expertise to figure out what is low and if it will someday sell high. People with limited time use mutual funds and hope that the fund manager is good at buying low and selling high.

Businesses can be bought and sold just like stock or mutual fund shares. An astute business person and investor can make a lot of money investing in small businesses - by buying them - and then working a turnaround in order to sell high.

The advantages over investing in stocks or bonds, directly or through mutual funds, is that you, he investor/manager, have much greater control over the outcome. You will understand the risks because you have done the work in assessing the purchase. Then you will be able to apply your special business talents to the turnaround. Or you will know what kind of expertise to retain or hire in order to make the turn-around work.

The process is relatively easy to understand and implement. You begin by prospecting for candidate companies. Then comes the task of screening the candidates for suitability. When you have narrowed the field, pick the most likely prospect and make a preliminary offer based on a 'first look.' (We'll talk more about how to do this, but you need to know at this point that the initial offer does not commit you to purchase the company.) This gives you the opportunity to get in and perform 'due diligence,' a careful collection of information and analysis of the facts. If due diligence convinces you that this is a reasonable turnaround candidate, then a final offer is made. You and your team will negotiate with the seller until a deal is made.

Now that the business is yours, you begin the turnaround course. This can take as little as a few months up to several years. A later chapter shows some of the more common turnaround strategies.

Finally, with the 'new' company in place, you switch roles and become the seller. But you will be a well-informed seller who can make a convincing case for the increased value of the business.

A quick note on tax policies and the buying and selling of small businesses. The U. S. Congress regularly tinkers with the tax code and one of the most common changes is in the capital gains tax rate. It is clearly advantageous to sell a business when the capital gains rate is low, and it may be easier to buy at that time since owners can be convinced that the timing is right. However, do not predicate your purchase and sale of small businesses on tax policy. You are betting on your financial and management skills, not the vagaries of the tax code.

There are three keys to making money in turn-arounds, and we will emphasize them throughout this book. Here they are:

- *Find a naive or desperate seller (or prepare to negotiate well with a sophisticated seller).*

- *Have a business plan and exit plan when you buy.*

- *Find the fastest turnarounds.*

Just a few preliminary words on each of these here.

Many - maybe most - small business owners are relatively naive about the true value of their companies. Those of us who have managed or owned a small business know that we spent most of our time dealing with the everyday problems. We focused on talking to customers, negotiating with suppliers, and supervising employees.

Not only that, but small business owners usually are experts in their field, whether it be model railroads for the hobby shop owner or printing technology for the print shop owner. Most of us are not trained in business fundamentals. We learned the business side while running the company we understood and loved. As a result, value is based on ego and heart. Investment bankers are just the opposite. They could care less about what kind of business they are buying; they focus on cash flow, net worth, and profitability. These investors need to know just enough about the business to understand how and why it makes money.

Then they establish a value.

Part of the naiveté of small business owners comes from the lack of a business plan and exit plan. All the books and experts recommend - strongly - that a business plan be created. Yet most of us struggle through the year with a vague idea about what we are trying to accomplish. A few may actually write out some goals. Yet in buying a business, it is extremely important to have a business plan *before* making the decision to purchase. Without the business plan there is no way to know if the value of the company can be increased in any reasonable time period.

The exit plan is just as important. What is an exit plan? A statement about how you want to get out of the business when it comes time to sell. Again, most small business owners don't think about this until it is too late. The exit plan is not a complicated document, several pages at most. We'll deal with it in more detail in a later chapter but basically it is a statement about how you want to relate to the business after it is sold and what kind of return you expect to get - and in what form.

Finally, you need to appreciate the fact that there are some businesses that can be turned around much more quickly than others. As a general rule, the more naive the current owner is about business and finance, the more rapidly you can shape up the company and sell it for a profit. Not only that, but you will be able to sell it for a sizable profit.

The concept of return on investment (ROI) is important here. If you invest $25,000 in a business and get $50,000 out of it two years later, you have realized a gain of $25,000 in the two years. That's a return of 41% compounded. If it takes four years to get the same return, the rate of return (ROI) drops to 19%. So the faster you can get your money out - assuming a decent increase in the investment - the better off you are.

Now that you have a preliminary understanding of the process and the critical elements in a good turn-around situation, there is one other matter to consider: you need to set up an advisory team to help you through the process. Two kinds of professionals are mandatory: a lawyer and an accountant. If you have a law degree and know something about business law, then you already know you will need an accountant. If you have a background in accounting and want to do turnarounds, you will need the expertise of a lawyer.

The accountant and lawyer are basic. A personal financial planner can be very useful in this process. After all, you are going to do these turnarounds in order to make money for yourself. The financial planner will be able to advise you on the best way to structure both the purchase and sale to maximize your personal return.

A good business broker can also be an asset. These people know what businesses are for sale and can save you a great deal of effort in prospecting and maybe even in screening. You always have to keep in mind, though, that the business broker wants you to buy as quickly as possible, that is how she or he maximizes return.

The advisory team should consist of:

• *A lawyer with a good business background.*

- *An accountant who specializes in business valuation and taxes.*

- *A financial planner who will look out for your personal financial interests.*

- *A business broker to aid in prospecting and screening.*

All four of these experts will be extremely useful in structuring the purchase and sale of the business.

You also need to know what I mean by a small business. The U.S. government defines a small business as one with 500 employees or fewer. That could be a business with annual sales of $20 million or more. I'm going to be dealing with much smaller businesses, let's say with annual sales ranging from $150,000 to $5 million. To benchmark these numbers, the typical one-person business, sometimes home-based, has annual sales of around $80,000. So a business with sales of $150,000 is still in all likelihood a one-person operation. Somewhere around $250,000 or more you are looking at several people and an office, shop, store, or other facility. Again, for comparison purposes, a typical fast food store or similar franchise operation probably grosses between $1 and $3 million a year. At $5 million, you may be looking at a company with 50 or more employees.

To buy into a small business you are going to need money. You would need that money if you were going to start a business. How much? Most people drastically underestimate what is required to start or buy a business. Some of the small part-time franchise deals that are available today require an investment of $10,000, maybe a little more or less. Full-time franchises or stand-alone businesses will require $20,000-50,000 at a minimum. That kind of money could buy you a business with gross sales of $100,000 to $500,000. To acquire a larger business could very well consume as much as $500,000. So your first step will be to find the money to invest. That is what you are doing: *Investing*. You are going to buy a business as an investment, turn it around, and then re-sell at a profit.

An important caveat here: don't believe the books, articles, or people who tell you that you can buy a business for little or nothing down and use the immense leverage to make a killing. Any business that can be purchased for very little down probably is in dire straits. Certainly you should use leverage, and we'll discuss how to structure the deal later in this book so that you don't have to buy all the assets for cash. But keep in mind the while some leverage is good, extreme leverage is not likely to happen in the real world. It makes for good reading but poor business practice.

The other key point to keep in mind is timing. Don't assume that because you have the money and the desire, a business for sale will turn up next month and you will own it a month later. Assume that you will spend at least six months and possibly more like a year prospecting before you find the right business. (For goodness sakes, don't buy the first one that comes along! This whole book is devoted to helping you buy the right business, not the most convenient one.) From there it could take another six months of negotiating and dealing with the paper work before closing.

The same holds true at the other end, when you are ready to sell. A buyer will not simply appear out of the blue to make you an offer you can't refuse. Allow a year or so to find the right buyer and again six months to consummate the deal.

In between you will be working as the owner/manager of the business. If you bought a business with a short turnaround time, you could put it back on the market within a year. In many cases, you will have to devote anywhere from two to five years before the company becomes salable at a price that earns you a decent return.

So what is the next step in this process, after you have put together an advisory team? *Start putting together the finances* needed to buy a likely acquisition. You may be one of the lucky (unlucky?) managers who took an early retirement from a major corporation and received a hefty buy-out or early retirement package. In that case, you may have enough dollars to finance the purchase on your own. Read no further in this chapter! Proceed to Chapter 2 and begin your search.

Suppose you don't have the money to buy anything larger than a small shoe repair shop in a small town (and you don't know anything about shoe repair and don't want to live in a small town). Maybe you have $5,000, $10,000, or even $20,000 that you are willing to invest. You need to go prospecting for money. Your first stop is family and friends. This is also a test for you. If you truly believe in your business skills, you should be able to ask these folks for money to support your enterprise. Of course, in this initial stage you don't know exactly what business you are going to buy, but your family and friends are not betting on that business, they are betting on you.

My rule of thumb in asking family and friends for capital is that you shouldn't ask any one person to put in more than you have invested. That seems to be an ethical position. Your risk should be as great or greater than theirs.

At this point you are only asking for a commitment, not the actual dollars. But you should have them sign some kind of document indicating their willingness to invest, say, $10,000. Find five of those people and you have $50,000 plus your own $15,000. With that amount of cash you can begin to do some serious looking.

There is more. Once you have your own commitment and that of your family and friends, you should begin to cultivate relationships with lawyers, accountants, financial planners, and business brokers. These are people who will help you prospect for small businesses up for sale, but they are also people who can assist you in raising more money. Business and estate planning lawyers, business and estate planning accountants, and financial planners usually deal with professionals such as doctors, dentists, managers, and other lawyers and accountants. Some of these professionals have money to invest. So you will be prospecting for potential investors.

At this point, however, don't start asking for names and money. Do your networking. Get to know these people. Let them get to know you. Your credibility as a business person is ultimately what will get you outside investment money, and the only way to build that credibility is by building relationships with key people. (Of course, it helps to have a background as an entrepreneur, owner, or manager of several small businesses in the past.)

You may, at some point in the future, want to finance an acquisition by raising equity, that is, selling shares in the business. You can do this through a private placement and avoid the hassles of an initial public offering. But you need to know the right people to do it. That is the reason for putting together a network of professionals who have many contacts in the local business community. It is absolutely vital to your ultimate success!

Now on to the 'meat' of the turnaround game which begins with the valuation of a business.

■

Chapter 2

VALUATION, ACCOUNTING, AND FINANCE FOR NON-ACCOUNTANTS

There is no way to find out if you are getting a good deal - in buying or selling a business - without some understanding of the ways in which companies are valued and the relationship of value to financial statements. You don't need to be an accountant or understand double-entry bookkeeping. You do need to understand how accountants function and how accounting systems are set up. The reason is simple: financial statements, as they are usually prepared and presented, are not a good basis for valuing a business. They need to be adjusted in a sensible and logical way to reflect value.

Accounting

Accounting consists of four tasks: recording, classifying, summarizing, and interpreting financial data in a business. Recording is a bookkeeping function. The ways in which accountants classify information begins the process of producing meaningful reports, and all of us in the business world should understand the fundamentals of financial classification, things like assets and liabilities. Those data are then summarized and the results become the "financials" of the business, the balance sheet and income or profit-and-loss (P&L) statement. The information on those two documents can then be interpreted, often in comparison to equivalent facts on similar businesses. That is known as financial statement analysis.

The people who set up and oversee accounting practices have defined the process of accounting as an art rather than a science. There is a lot of judgment involved in the classifying, summarizing, and interpreting of business financial data.

Because accounting is an art, its practitioners are cautioned, by the professional code, to be *conservative* in their judgments. Given a choice between an optimistic and pessimistic way to view the numbers, the accountant should take the more cautious pessimistic position. This guideline comes about because the *public accountant* (that's a CPA) is relied upon to produce information useful to lenders and investors who do not want to lend or put their money into an enterprise that has problems.

To further provide comparability, the accounting profession has set up Generally Accepted Accounting Principles (GAAP). These principles insure that the data relating to one firm are at least approximately similar to those from another.

The most important single fact to keep in mind in looking over financial statements is this: accounting deals with costs. What you see on the balance sheet as the dollars in inventory is what the inventory cost the business, usually with some kind of depreciation included. It is not what the inventory could be sold for, but what it cost. What you see on the balance sheet as fixed assets are what those items cost - when purchased and minus depreciation since their purchase. That number probably bears little or no resemblance to what the fixed assets are worth on today's market. They could be valued higher or lower.

Remember that accounting:

> *is an art*
>
> *leans towards the conservative side*
>
> *uses costs - not value - in its reports.*

All of this results in information which is useful to lenders and investors, but that information has to be looked at critically and adjusted intelligently to arrive at *the value of the company.*

Valuation

So how much is a company worth? That depends! Of course, that's always the answer to complex questions. Before getting into valuation methods, let's get one thing straight. The price of acquisition is not necessarily the value of the company. A price is agreed upon by a seller and buyer. In a practical sense, that is what the company is worth. It is whatever those two parties are able to establish between themselves.

An important principle for you - and a very elementary one - is that *you want to pay a price below the value of the business*. Buy low; sell high is still the basic dictum of all good investments.

One other warning before we get into the details of valuation. Beware of any accountant or financial planner who uses a 'quicky formula" to get an estimate of value. For example, there are formulas that multiply the net profit of a company by a factor of five or seven or ten, depending on the kind of business, to get a value number.

With all of that in mind, how do sellers value their businesses? One flip answer is: poorly. Remember that you are looking for a naive seller, and that is someone who doesn't understand the value of her or his business. Someone who doesn't understand what we just explained about accounting. "Whatever is on the balance sheet is what the business is worth." Not true! In the next chapter, we'll discuss the characteristics of the naive seller in more detail.

Four valuation methods will be reviewed here: net worth or "book value," income or cash flow stream value, liquidation value, and replacement value.

Probably the most common seller valuation - as just hinted - is based on net worth or "book value." After all, the owner of the company has been working for years and looking at the balance sheet every month or every quarter, certainly every year. The number at the bottom of that page is what the business is worth. A book value of $235,000. "That's what I'll sell for."

The advantage to you as a buyer is that book value may well be below real value because of the conservatism and the cost basis of accounting. (That's why understanding the philosophy of accounting is important.) How do you take advantage of this? Smart buyers perform a detailed business analysis which involves recasting the balance sheet and income statement. Those are the subject of later sections, but they represent the way a sophisticated buyer is able to find "good deals."

Another factor to keep in mind is that book value represents the historical value of the business, that is, the results of prior operations. The owner is selling the past. You are not - should not be - buying the past. *You are buying the future of the company.* Thus, in a later section of this chapter, we will show how to value a business based on its future cash flow, not its present book value.

Rarely will you be able to buy a business for less than its book value. If you do, it will result from a careful sales job on the present owner. You will have to convince him or her through analysis and documentation that the balance sheet numbers are wrong. And that is a politically difficult maneuver because manager-owners of small businesses have a lot of ego tied up in the financial results of years past.

Now a deal can be structured so that it appears to be worth the book value of the company when in fact it is not. This is also the subject of a later chapter.

Only a desperate seller will agree to a price below book value. More will be said about desperate sellers in the next chapter, but they usually are in personal financial difficulty and need money quickly to get out of trouble.

More common is the seller who wants book value plus a premium. There are two rationales used by owners for the premium, neither one based on good financial or business principles: "I should get a premium because of all the hard work I have put into this place" or "I should get a premium because I need the money to ____ (retire, live it up, start a new business)." These are purely psychological reasons for the extra money. But they can be hard to dispel. Sellers who want a premium without a sound business rationale should be avoided!

Assessing Book Value

The net asset value of a business is most useful in cases where the company is asset-rich: meaning fixed assets such as land, buildings, equipment, facilities. Actually, the price of many businesses is due more to income and cash flow than book value. But as I just got done saying, book value is what owners use as a gauge. So you need to start with an analysis of the book value of the company and what it means.

This should happen before you make an initial offer. The owner should be willing to show you the financials on the company based on a letter of intent from you and a confidentiality agreement which you sign.

To assess book value, you need to re-cast the balance sheet. The typical CPA cannot do this because it would violate the rules and practices of the accounting profession. Maybe an accountant working for you can assist in the process.

An outline of a balance sheet is shown on the next page. It is presented to illustrate some of the kinds of adjustments that need to be made. The balance sheet for a particular business will probably differ from the example below.

Here is the outline of a balance sheet:

Assets

Current assets
  Cash and equivalents
  Accounts receivable
  Inventory (or work in process)
  Note receivable from owner
Fixed assets
  Equipment
  Building and land

Liabilities

Current liabilities
  Accounts payable
  Taxes payable
  Loan payable to owner
    (current year)
Long-term liabilities
  Loan payable to owner

Owners' Equity

Capital stock
Retained earnings

We haven't put numbers in to avoid getting into computations. Description will be enough to show you how a balance sheet can be re-cast.

The book value of the business is found by taking the total assets and subtracting the liabilities. The number will be the same as the sum of the capital stock and retained earnings.

Here are the adjustments that should be made to the outlined balance sheet:

- Delete the cash and equivalents.

- Analyze the accounts receivable to see how "good" they are.

- Analyze the inventory or work-in-process to see how "good" they are.

- Find the fair market value of the fixed assets.

- Delete the building and land from the fixed assets.

- Net out the notes receivable from and payable to the owner and place them in the Owners' Equity section.

Here's the rationale for each of these moves.

The cash and cash equivalents are normally not sold with the business. The current owner retains those amounts. From the buyer's standpoint, there isn't much reason to buy cash. You are paying cash for cash. You can do that at any bank. You want your money to go toward acquisition of other assets.

The analysis of the accounts receivable and inventory is very important to arrive at a realistic estimate of the value of the business. (Incidentally, work-in-process is used in manufacturing to show the costs of the parts, assemblies, and so on which are in the shop or on the shelves and not yet part of a complete product; when the product is complete, it goes into inventory.)

Normally you will not be able to verify the accounts receivable and inventory until you have made an offer and are in the process of due diligence. But you can make some preliminary estimates based on industry standards and your own past experience. You will make these preliminary estimates in order to develop an offer, but you will reserve the right to adjust the offer *after you have performed due diligence.*

On the subject of receivables, eventually you will want what is known as an "aged receivables" list. that is, a list showing who owes what and how long it has been outstanding. Rarely are all of the receivables listed on the balance sheet collectable. So you need to factor those down by some amount.

When you get the aged receivables list during due diligence and prior to you final offer, you need to adjust them. One way to do this, as an example, is to reduce the 30-day receivables to 95% of their current value, 30-60-day receivables to 85%, and so on. You would probably ignore - reduce to zero - and receivables older than 120 days.

With inventory, the critical issue is how much of it is salable within a reasonable period of time? Most businesses carry at least some inventory that is simply never going to go to a customer. That amount needs to be written off.

Now comes the issue of fixed assets. Remember that they are carried on the books at cost minus depreciation. You need to get an estimate of the current fair market value. To do that, you usually have to go to a catalog or dealer in used equipment who can provide an estimate.

Now why delete the value of the building and land from the re-cast balance sheet? The sage advice of many experts in buying businesses is to make the real estate a separate deal, if you want it at all. The reason is quite simple. Real estate is an entirely different issue than the operating business. The value of the land and building may increase or decrease depending on the local real estate market and has nothing to do with how you run the business. Remember that you are betting on your ability to turn the operating business around, not on your ability to out-guess the real estate market. (We'll temper that statement in a later chapter.)

There is another business reason for not buying the real estate. If you are going to invest in an operating company, you should apply the money invested on items that will generate income in the future. That is the "operating" part of the operating company. A building and land do not contribute to the income or profitability of the business.

In a recent case, the book value of the company was $442,000 in round numbers. The adjustments made during due diligence reduced that to $332,000. Because there was real estate involved, the owner proceeded with the sale and retained the land and building and leased the latter to the new owner.

Finally, in our fictitious example, the company's owner had to borrow money from the company (note receivable from owner under Assets) and had lent the company money (note payable to owner under Liabilities).The two notes should be combined and put under Owner's Equity because they have nothing to do with how a new owner would operate the business. In fact, the normal procedure at closing would be for the owner to pay off the note to the company and be paid off for the note from the company. So that needs to be done in your analysis of the balance sheet. You aren't going to "buy" either note.

Assessing Cash Flow Potential

The second way to value a business is by looking at the income it generates. This is done by looking over the P&L or income statement.

Here it is important to realize that many small businesses are operated in a way to minimize profit. Why? Because with a "C" corporation, the dividends are taxed to the shareholder after the corporation pays its income tax. Double taxation. So the managers of a "C" corporation usually try to work things out so that the net income reported on the P&L is low.

Even in sole proprietorships, partnerships, and "S" corporations - where double taxation is not a problem - the owners frequently minimize profits by taking money out in tax-free or tax-deferred methods allowed under the income tax code.

This means that the purchaser must look at the cash flow of the company, not just the net profit from the income statement.

A typical income statement looks something like this:

Sales
Cost of Goods Sold
    Wages
    Purchased items
    Subcontracts
Gross Profit
Fixed Expenses
    Rent
    Utilities
    Insurance, business
    Insurance, key man
    Telephone
    Maintenance and repair
    Advertising
    Travel and auto expense
Net Profit
Interest expense
Taxes
Earnings after taxes and interest

What should you look for? Here are some basics, and your accountant and financial planner can help you decipher more. Analyze the P&L statement for owner perks, such things as life, health and accident, disability, and other forms of insurance. Owners are also able to use corporate money to pay for dental work, glasses, prescriptions and similar medical expenses which may not be covered under the health and accident insurance plan. There may also be a company car, owned by the business, which the owner uses. Another common benefit of the owner is travel to trade shows, professional meetings, and similar events. These are usually held in good geographical locations and that permit the owner to enjoy the benefits of the climate, shopping, or entertainment at the convention site.

Also check the salary paid to the owner. In some cases it is well above the industry average for a hired manager in the same position. Any excess is cash that could be applied to product improvement, better marketing, or other investments to improve the state of the business. Dividends are a cash drain on the company, and if you buy it and re-organize it or run it differently, the dividend cash can also be used in the turnaround effort.

Interest charges need to be assessed. If you can operate the business with less or no borrowed money, the amount of interest will be less and you can use the resulting cash in your turnaround activities.

Your accountant can also look at depreciation charges. They subtract from the apparent profitability of a business but do not, in fact, result in less money in the till. Such charges are quite literally on paper.

After going through this process, you and your advisory team will be able to sum the reported net profit plus all of the other current cash flow items to obtain a total. In one recent case, we showed that a company reporting net profits averaging $20,000 a year was actually throwing off over $100,000 a year to its owner and managers.

How do we find a valuation from the cash flow data? The premise is that you are buying an income or cash stream for some period of time in the future when you purchase a business. If a company is generating $100,000 a year in cash, then in five years you will have gotten $500,000. The owner, relying on the balance sheet, thinks the business is worth $250,000. That is good deal for the buyer, with certain caveats.

The way in which cash flow projections are used in valuation is called *discounted cash flow (DCF)*. Appendix E shows how DCF is calculated. This is a process that involves mathematical calculations which we won't go into here (there are lots of good books on financial analysis that show how to compute DCF). But, again, you need to understand the principles.

The first elementary step in understanding discounted cash flow is the idea that money available today is worth more than money provided at some future date. The reason is that you could be earning interest, dividends, or some other kind of income from the money if you had it today. If someone were to give you $1000 today and you invested it at 10%, then in one year you would have $1100. If that same someone gave you an interest-free note for the money in one year, you would have $1000, not $1100.

The interest rate used in the DCF calculations is called the *discount* rate. (This is not in any way related to inflation rates but rather to the income you could have earned if you had the money in hand.) What discount rate should you or your financial advisors use in computing the value of a company? The discount rate should be the same as that for *an investment with equal risk*. If you are looking at a company that is a basket case, in really poor condition, and there is real risk in trying to get it turned around, then you should use a discount rate of 20-30%, maybe even higher. On the other hand, if it is performing well and only needs minor tuning, you can use a discount rate of 10-12%.

You can find the return rate on various kinds of investments from the *Wall Street Journal* or other financial publications. Just look at the return over reasonable periods of time on U.S. Treasury notes, common stocks, corporate bonds, municipal bonds, and other kinds of investment vehicles. As a kind of benchmark, the U.S. stock markets have returned around 11% to investors over long periods of time which include some big bull and big bear markets.

There are two other factors that influence the DCF calculation outcome. One of those is the *expected flow of cash*. We just finished discussing how to re-cast the income statement of a small business to get an estimate of cash - in the past. Your problem is to estimate the cash flow in the future. To get a valid estimate, you really need to create a preliminary business plan (see the chapter on this subject later in this book).

You can create three estimates of the value of a company from the re-cast income statement. It may be reasonable to assume that the business can at least continue throwing off the cash it has in the past.

If that is true, then use that number for the DCF computation. As a worst case, you could assume that the cash flow will decrease from its current level to zero in, say, ten years. And, in terms of a best case, you can increase the cash flow on some reasonable basis for the next five to ten years because you are confident of your ability to turn the business around.

The final factor in the equation is the *length of time* you can expect the cash flow to continue. We had to deal with that already in the preceding paragraph. Some businesses have an almost infinite life. Funeral homes are an example. People will continue to need the services of the mortician and funeral director for as far in the future as we can see. Styling and barber shops are another example as are tax preparation services. On the other hand, there are some businesses that are fairly short-lived. Videotape rental operations started in the late 1970s but their business is likely to hold steady or decline in the future because of the onset of 500-channel cable, interactive computer media hardware and software, and other new technologies. At the time this is being written, specialty coffee outlets are springing up in many strip malls, but the fad of high-priced latte(and cappuccino could disappear in a year or two.

To review, the value of a business can be calculated using discounted cash flow methods, and the range of values will depend on:

> the projected cash flow,
>
> the discount rate used in the calculations,
>
> the time period employed.

The calculation can be performed on any standard financial calculator or on a computer spreadsheet.

Liquidation and Replacement Value Estimates

There are two other standard methods for obtaining business valuations. The liquidation estimate is just what it implies. You sit down and figure out what you could get by selling off the assets of the company and paying off the liabilities. This is of little use to someone who wants to do a turnaround. But it does represent a benchmark lowest value.

Replacement value is just as self-evident. You compute what it could cost to create the business from scratch. Add up all the money it would take to buy equipment and inventory, hire people, obtain all the licenses, and create a marketing and sales effort. You need to include the salary you would pay yourself and others during the time the business is being created and built, that is, before it begins to generate any income or profit. In most cases, the replacement value is much higher than the book value or cash flow valuation methods, so it represents a high benchmark value.

Using the Valuation Estimates

Okay, so now we have at least two valuations - net asset value and cash flow value - and maybe two more - liquidation and replacement value. What do we do?

The first step is to compare the re-cast net worth to that shown on the latest balance sheet for the business. The best scenario occurs if the re-cast value is more than the book value because you can buy below the real value. That may not happen very often.

The next step is to compare the valuations obtained by re-casting the balance sheet and by performing the income stream (discounted cash flow) analysis. Ideally, the latter - cash flow stream - will exceed the net worth. Why ideally? Because as we noted earlier, most naive sellers based their valuation on net worth. If the current owner is willing to sell at book value and you know that the income stream is actually worth more, it is to your advantage.

Finally, compare both the re-cast net worth and income stream valuations to those you got from estimating the liquidation and replacement numbers.

The best situation is if the numbers arrange themselves like this:

Replacement value - high

Income stream value - next highest

Book value - next lowest

Liquidation value - lowest

Incidentally, if the liquidation value is higher than the current book value of the company, it is a good deal! Even if you can't turn it around, you can liquidate it and make a profit. Just be aware that this probably happens only once in a few million business deals!

If you can start a company cheaper than you can buy it, then start it!

From here - the basics of valuation, accounting, and finance - we need to get on with the practical issues of finding candidate businesses and sellers.

Chapter 3

FINDING COMPANIES TO BUY

You should have a basic understanding, from the previous two chapters, of the process involved in making money through small business turnarounds and the some of the financial considerations involved. Here is the really practical issue: Where do we find companies for sale? How do we go about contacting them? And how do we get preliminary information to know if they are candidates for turnaround?

Before launching into those matters, you need to be aware of one important point. Finding and buying a good small business will take some time. The advice to owners who are selling a company is that it takes a year or two to complete the deal after the business is put on the market. You should figure on about a year of negotiations after you have located some good candidate companies, and it could take six months to several years to find one or more good candidates. This is not a get-rich-quick scheme!

In fact, you need to be warned that one of the dangers in this game is to acquire a company before you have done all the work needed to ensure it is a decent turnaround candidate. Here is a "stitch in time saves nine" situation.

The overall process for making money with small business turnarounds was outlined in Chapter 1: prospecting, screening, offer, due diligence, negotiation, and then the agreement. After that you perform your magic to make the business more profitable and put it back on the market.

Creating Lists of Prospects

There are two ways to go about the prospecting and screening process, and you probably should use both. The first is to get a list of all the companies that are for sale in the geographic area in which you are interested. Presumably you want to buy a business in the area where you are currently living, and that makes the most sense because it is where you have the best network of contacts. (Buying a business in another locale can be tricky because you will have to rely on brokers, lawyers, accountants, and so on in that area, whom you probably don't know all that well, and the travel to and from can get expensive.) So you have a list of companies for sale, and including bankruptcies. Later in this chapter we'll discuss how to generate these lists. Now out of all the companies available, you need to quickly identify the ones that match your business background and talents.

The second great danger is to get into a business that you don't understand. Peter Lynch, the investment guru, is emphatic about investing in the shares of businesses you understand. That goes double for buying a business. If you have never been involved in the hospitality industry then don't try to buy a motel or restaurant or travel agency. The only way to do that would be to a have partner who understands the specific business while you provide the business smarts.

After creating the list of available businesses, make a second list of all the businesses of the type that you want to acquire. Styling lounges? Machine shops? Whatever, get that list together also. The reason is that some of those businesses might be "purchasable." Some owners are on the verge of selling but haven't quite made the decision yet. If someone were to approach them with an indication of interest, they might go over the edge and entertain an offer.

There are a number of ways to generate prospect lists:

- Business and professional contacts

- Friends, relatives, and neighbors

- Bankers and other lenders

- Chambers of commerce

- Economic development staffs in local and state government

- Real estate firms (in small cities and towns)

- Business brokers

- Want ads in newspapers or magazines on businesses for sale

- A want ad soliciting businesses for sale

Remember that at this point you just want a list of possibilities, and the more ways you use to generate that list, the bigger it will be.

Let's review each of these sources of information. Start with personal contacts, people you already know. First among these are business and professional contacts. You should know some people in the business world, specifically in the general area in which you want to buy, for example, retail or manufacturing. Let those people know that you are looking for a company to buy. They go to meetings and to lunch with other business people. In the process, they may have heard of something. You can ask them to mention that you are in the market to buy a business. Sooner or later you will get some good contacts in this way, and they could be exactly the kind of company you are looking for.

Don't overlook family, friends, and neighbors. Let them know what you are trying to do. They should be encouraged to mention your goal of buying a small business to their acquaintances. This is the essence of networking, to have people contacting other people for you.

Another source of information about companies that might be sold is bankers and business lenders. Some banks specialize in small business accounts and loans. You can usually find out about them through the Small Business Administration office in your area. If you are looking at a small town setting, then the local bank is usually heavily into small business lending.

Now bankers are not going to offer you a list of names of small businesses that might be for sale. That would violate their ethics. However, you can contact the bank - the president and key vice presidents in the case of a small bank, one or two or the loan officers in a larger bank - and simply indicate that you are in the market to purchase a small business. You should indicate the kind of small business, your ability to see the deal through, and your business background. There is a constant turnover of ownership of small businesses and the bank, as a lending agency, wants to make sure that a business that is in the doldrums or even in trouble will have an energetic and competent new owner. So they may suggest to an owner sometime in the next months that they know of an interested buyer. Then they will let you and the owner get together. The bank, clearly, will not function as a broker.

Here is a handy hint. Before contacting a banker, lender, chamber of commerce staff member, real estate broker, business broker, or other source, I would strongly urge you to compose a letter of introduction. What should it say? Something like this:

"Dear _____:

I am searching for a small business to buy. Because of my background, I want to purchase a _____ business (fill in the blank with manufacturing, retail, personal service, or whatever and add more details about what you are looking for if that is appropriate).

My plan is to perform a careful assessment of any candidate company and to develop a business plan if one does not already exist or is out of date. I believe as a professional business manager and that I can improve the performance of the right company in the right situation.

At present, I have $XX,XXX to invest in the right situation. This money represents my own money plus commitments from _____ (fill in the blank and add details as needed).

My strengths as a business person are _____ (again, the blanks), and I will supplement those skills with a professional team including an attorney, accountant, financial planner, and _____ (more blanks to fill in).

I would appreciate knowing of any businesses that might for sale or, alternatively, indicating my interest to a business owner of your acquaintance who might be willing to discuss selling.

Very truly yours,

_____ "

You should provide such a letter to business attorneys, accountants, financial planners, or other professional who might have contact with small business owners. These could very well be the same people who you contacted earlier in a preliminary networking efforts and as potential sources of investment money.

Chambers of commerce may also be a source of information on local small businesses. Once again, these people have interest in seeing that existing businesses prosper and grow. They can inform a member that someone is looking to buy a business and serve, in this way, as an initial link.

Many communities and areas have a Small Business Development Center (SBDC) sponsored by the Small Business Administration (SBA). The SBDC is often located in a college or university. The staff will have some knowledge of local business conditions and contact with small business owners. These staff members can also act as initial links between you and an owner.

Business brokers are an obvious source of information. You need to be aware that, as in all businesses, there are reputable and less reputable brokers. You should indicate by means of a letter your interest in acquiring a small business and the letter should include the kind of business and the amount of money you have to invest. A good business broker will help a seller prepare the business for sale, and that is something you don't necessarily want. On the other hand, some sellers simply don't do what the broker suggests - or do it halfheartedly - so you can still find good deals by working through a broker.

The enormous advantage of working through a broker or brokers is that they have the listing readily at hand. A good broker will have numerous businesses listed and you can pick and choose to some extent. Be aware, however, that business brokers are not like real estate firms: they don't have multiple listing services. So you need to contact several brokers - or all of them - in your area to have access to most of the companies that are listed.

Real estate firms in small cities and towns often serve as business brokers. Motels, restaurants, bars, barbershops and styling lounges, liquor stores, and small retail shops frequently are listed through a real estate firm. This happens because the principal asset of the business is the building and land. The owner adds in the inventory and/or equipment to get a sale price. Your advantage here is that the real estate agent normally is not very knowledgeable in business valuations. The agent and broker will know the value of the land and building but not of the operating business. So you may have an opportunity to find the right kind of business this way.

Bankruptcy court is yet another source of information. Some bankruptcies are not worth looking at. There are few assets and the business has been run into the ground. However, there are some "good" bankruptcies, and we'll deal with this issue more in a later chapter. You should understand at this point that some businesses go into bankruptcy while still viable. A common reason for declaring bankruptcy is a lack of cash. When the business runs out of cash and can't pay its creditors, one recourse is to go to bankruptcy court.

All bankruptcies are filed in the federal bankruptcy court in your area, and the information on these companies is available for review. So you not only get a listing of the companies but also what they do and their current financial status.

Want ads for "businesses for sale" appear in newspapers on a regular basis. These may be useful to you but you should be careful in following up on them. Any halfway knowledgeable business owner will use networking, a business broker, and other means to announce the intention to sell. Putting an ad in the local paper, unless it is a real estate deal, is not smart, mainly because the owner will get all kinds of responses most of which will not be from legitimate buyers.

A want ad soliciting businesses for sale may pay off in some communities and areas and certainly would be worth the small investment required for such an ad. Some business owners do read the want ads, and you could get a lead or two in this way.

Since you intend to be a professional buyer and seller of small businesses, the best way to proceed is to use as many of the suggestions listed above as possible. Use your network of relatives, friends, and neighbors as well as business and professional acquaintances. Talk to people in the local chamber of commerce and the SBDC in your area. Write letters of introduction to local bankers and then go in for an appointment. Check in with the business brokers and, if appropriate, real estate brokers. Go to the bankruptcy court and look over the listing there. Put an ad in the paper, and read the want ads to see what kinds of small businesses are advertised for sale. Get as many people and agencies working for you as possible.

Keep a list of the prospective companies. Follow-up on them and maintain a record of the results. After a few months you will begin to get a feel for what works and what doesn't in your community or area.

The Special Case of Bankruptcies

Ordinarily you might not think about buying a company that is in the midst of bankruptcy, but that is a premature judgment, if you have made it. Some of those companies are logical candidates for your turnaround efforts, and they have the advantage that they are all listed in one place: the federal bankruptcy court in your jurisdiction.

Understand, first, the kinds of bankruptcies and the process involved in filing for bankruptcy. Chapter 7, as you probably know, is a filing for liquidation. The assets will be sold, and the proceeds distributed to the creditors. You are more interested in the Chapter 11 cases where the company has filed for reorganization, meaning that someone thinks it can be saved. Generally, the owner and management file for this kind of bankruptcy, although creditors can force it.

When a company files for Chapter 11 it continues to operate as before with just a few restrictions. The management cannot take on more debt, make large investments, hire additional management personnel, or take certain other extraordinary actions. Everything else stays the same. Workers keep working. Customers keep on buying. The accountant keeps the books. And so on.

Shortly after filing, the company must provide the bankruptcy court with a Schedule of Assets and Liabilities and a Statement of Financial Affairs for a Debtor Engaged in Business. These documents relate to the condition of the business at the time of filing, and if the filing occurred quite a while ago, the current condition could be different. However, the company also has to provide the court with monthly financial reports. So not only do you have a convenient list of businesses that might be available for purchase but also some initial information on their financial plight.

The businesses in bankruptcy range from real basket cases to ones that just ran into a single piece of bad luck, admittedly major bad luck. Frequently a cause for filing for bankruptcy is a shortage of cash: creditors simply cannot be paid in a timely fashion. So there is hope!

Preliminary Screening

Your initial list contains the names and addresses of companies and, preferably, the name of the owner. If not, you should have a contact name at the company in the case of hired non-owner management.

The next step is to send a brief letter indicating an interest for those companies where you are not dealing with a business or real estate broker. In those latter situations, the broker will make the initial contact, usually not disclosing your name until later. The brokers, by the way, will want to "qualify" you, that is, make sure you are a legitimate buyer and have the money to do the deal.

In your introductory letter, you should express your interest and your willingness to sign a non-disclosure (or confidentiality) agreement. Your intent at this point is to obtain preliminary information on the company, and the owner does not want that data spread around the local area.

If the business is for sale, the owner - or broker - should have some of this preliminary information available for you. That would include, as a minimum, the following:

- Balance sheets for the prior 3-5 years

- Income statement for the prior 3-5 years

- Brief statement of the nature of business and its products and markets

- Company history

If the business is not for sale but you think the owner might be ready to sell or you have gotten some information indicating that she has thought about it, then you will not get the information listed above right at the beginning. In that case, you need to write a letter of introduction including the statement that you are in the market to buy a small company and would like to explore the possibility.

Assuming that you get a positive response in a follow-up phone call, you should set up a preliminary meeting. And if you have gotten the information listed previously and are interested in a business, you also need to set up a preliminary meeting. This meeting is critical! Most buyers don't realize that many a deal has gone sour because of bad "chemistry" between the buyer and seller. This is a time to be reserved and polite while still showing real interest in the owner and the business.

In the case of a bankruptcy, you should approach the owner as a potential 'white knight' who might be able to help her or him out of the current situation. State initially that you are an investor, and avoid coming right out and saying you might want to buy the company. After all, the owner is in reorganization in hopes of turning the business around without selling it.

Your task is to obtain information. Therefore, you need to crank up your listening skills. Ask questions, particularly open-ended questions: why? how? when? who? what? Avoid questions that can be answered "yes" or "no." Show interest in the owner. Ask about family. Comment on pictures or decorations in the office. This is a time to be a good conversationalist.

The last thing you should do is come charging in like a human tornado. Don't critique the way the business looks or is operated. Don't talk about your own big successes - and make the owner look small or bad. Don't ask leading questions like "What is so bad about this place that you want to sell?" And, my goodness, don't make it into an interview with a list of questions!

Now being a good conversationalist does mean talking about yourself to some extent. The best advice is to be direct and honest. And that means, at some point, bringing up some problems you have had in the past in running a business or a failure that you experienced. Human nature is such that if you reveal this kind of information, the other person is likely to do the same. And you will gain valuable insight into the owner and the business.

The owner should ask you to sign a confidentiality agreement at some point in this initial meeting. Read it over carefully to indicate that you are meticulous about that kind of thing. But unless there are some really bizarre conditions in it, sign the agreement. This is a gesture of goodwill on your part and will make the owner feel better about you. If there is something that bothers you, say so and indicate that you want your lawyer to look it over. But that is rare. After all, there is no reason why you should want to disclose information about this other person's business.

Once that is out of the way - or you may have signed such an agreement through a broker - it is time to move on to substantive matters. You should get a tour of the facility. You should have access to standard marketing and sales brochures. You should be able to look at the offices. You probably will not be allowed to talk to the employees at this point. After all, they could become tense and exhibit lower morale if they think the current owner is selling.

As soon as this initial meeting and tour are over, write out your notes on the overall impression you received.

Now comes the part where you apply your knowledge of small business financials or rely on your accountant and financial planner to do it for you. The process outlined here is very similar to that used by analyst for mutual funds and financial advisory firms. The information in Chapter 2 is relevant here. You need to re-cast the balance sheet to get a more accurate representation of the net worth of the company. In particular, you and your team want to look for undervalued and so-called "hidden" assets. These come in many forms. For example, a long-term lease on favorable terms is a hidden asset. So are patents, trademarks, and copyrights which normally are not carried on the balance sheet. The same goes for trade secrets. These are items that you can find out about only by talking with the owner since they are not listed anywhere on a financial document.

Any assets that have been depreciated by the accountant or bookkeeper but which have a fair market value above their depreciated value also should be considered. This is particularly true, as we noted earlier, about real estate, and that is a subject to which we will return in a later chapter.

You should try to come up with two numbers in your initial analysis of the business. The first is simply a re-cast balance sheet net worth for the company.

This may be higher or lower than the net worth shown on the financials you were given. The second number is a net worth obtained by adding in any undervalued or hidden assets. As noted previously, you are looking for situations where the owner's balance sheet shows a number lower than either or both of yours. In such a case, you can buy the company at the apparent book value and will acquire some additional assets "for free."

The second part of the analysis process is the review of the income statements for the last three to five years. There are several things to look for here. First, is the income stream steady, increasing, decreasing, or erratic? If it is steady, you can assume more of the same for the next three to five years as long as the overall outlook for that kind of business and for the economy is steady as well. A decreasing income or cash flow stream spells trouble. You need to look at the reason for the decrease and, in addition, ask the owner for an explanation. Obviously if it keeps decreasing you are buying something that is losing value. Not a good idea! Some businesses exhibit an erratic cash flow stream. This is particularly true, as an example, in manufacturing or wholesaling where the company depends on several large customers. The ups and down associated with the customers are reflected in the small business books.

You are looking for a business that has an increasing cash flow stream. Of course, you need to know why and how the increase is occurring and particularly if it due to some quirk that will reverse in the next few years. But assuming that the increase is real and can be anticipated to continue, the business is probably worth more than one with a steady stream for the clear reason that you are buying something that is increasing in value.

There needs to be a comparison between the book value of the company and the value obtained from the cash flow stream projection. Here, you want a business that is worth more in terms of income stream than on the balance sheet. You should be able to buy for the book value but actually purchase something worth more.

In summary, you should look for a business that has:

- undervalued or hidden assets,

- a book value that is below the valuation obtained from

- analyzing income and cash flow stream, and

- a projected increase in income stream over the next three to five years.

The last item suggests one other matter which needs to be addressed. Suppose the business is showing a steady cash flow stream for the last five years. The key question is this: can you do anything to improve it over the next year or two? That is truly the $64,000 question in many cases. You should be able to give a positive response if you buy the right business, and we'll talk about how to find companies that are ripe for a turnaround a little later in this book. After all, this is a book about turnarounds, and that suggests that you ought to be able to increase the income stream with some relatively straightforward business strategies.

Turning a small business around, if done properly, should include a business plan, and in the course of doing your initial assessment of the company, you should be thinking in broad terms about the elements of a business plan: marketing and sales, product development, costs and cost containment, personnel and staffing, and so on. Most promising turnaround candidates require a new and better approach to management and marketing. These usually involve the least need for cash investment and can produce a large payoff in a reasonably short period of time. More about that later.

Remember that your goal is to buy at a discount. The most probable selling price by a naive seller is likely to be the current book value of the company. If you can buy at that level and there are undervalued or hidden assets, there is an income stream that exceeds the book value, and particularly if the cash flow stream is increasing, then you have a situation where you are buying low and will be able to sell high. And the nice thing about it is that you won't have to wait for the stock market to find out about it as happens when you buy a stock. You can do it on your own.

The "formal" information about the business - financials, history, products and markets - is obviously important, but there is something equally, if not more, important for you to discover: why is the owner selling? There are good reasons and bad ones. We will talk more about owners, particularly naive owners, in the next chapter, but you need to know, at this point, what to look for as you engage in your initial contacts with the owner.

The most common reason for selling, as mentioned earlier, is boredom. There is only so much you can do with a small business. There are limits to how much it can grow because there are limits to the resources. Small business owners get restless. They want to try their hand at some other business or the same business but in another locale. A bored seller is okay.

A second common reason for selling is burn out. You simply cannot get away from a small business. It is always there. So, most owners find that staying with the company gets harder and harder as time goes on. The time period varies but generally runs from seven to twelve years. At that point, the owner is ready to get out, even if it is just to move on to another small business.

A third common - and good - reason for selling is age. The owner wants to retire but doesn't want to shut down the business. So he or she looks for a buyer. This even happens to a family business if none of the children want to carry it on.

Along the same lines, disability or illness are perfectly good reasons to bail out of a business. If the owner simply cannot put in the time or devote the energy to the business, it is time to cash out.

A few owners need to get out because of personal financial problems, and selling the business is one way to generate cash to pay off the IRS or those credit card bills or the back child support or alimony. Such an owner can be easy to work with because of the need to get the cash, but on the other hand could also want more money and in cash than you are willing to pay. It is legitimate, by the way, to ask the owner for her or his personal financial statements along with those of the company. One reason is that they give you a better idea of what the person has gotten out of the business in terms of salary and benefits. But the information can really help you in understanding whether the owner needs to get out for financial reasons.

The worst reasons for selling a business, quite obviously, are that the whole thing is in really bad shape or is about to be slapped with a lawsuit. Of course, no one is going to tell you this. So if you walk into a business being run by a 40-something owner who doesn't seem bored and doesn't seem to have any plans for the immediate future, such as starting another business, beware!

Again, let's make sure that you know it is perfectly okay to ask the current owner why he or she wants to sell. That is legitimate information for you, and the legitimate seller will be more than happy to discuss it with you.

Let's review briefly. You should eliminate from your search any businesses that:

- Have a net worth on the books that is much higher than your re-cast book value;

- Have a cash flow stream worth less than the re-cast book value;

- Have a decreasing or erratic income stream over the past three to five years;

- Whose owner is not upfront with you about why she or he wants out.

We will provide other screens in a subsequent chapter, but these are basic to the process of initial screening.

■

Chapter 4

FINDING A NAIVE OR DESPERATE SELLER... AND HOW TO PREPARE TO NEGOTIATE WITH A SOPHISTICATED SELLER

This chapter raises some ethical questions. The title implies that you can take advantage of a naive or desperate seller. That is true to some extent. Every business has a fair market value. Your goal is to buy below the fair market value. Ideally, you would like to buy a business low enough that you could turn right around and re-sell at a profit. That isn't likely to happen. But you can find some good deals.

In the business world we are familiar with the old caveat of "buyer beware." There should be an equivalent "seller beware," whether selling product, service, or a business. It is up to the seller to ascertain the fair market value or her or his business and then try to get that price.

It is up to you to decide whether or not you want to take advantage of someone who is naive or desperate. I also need to point out that naive and desperate sellers can also ask far too much for their businesses. A naive owner may really believe a balance sheet that is not an accurate reflection of worth. A desperate seller may have to get a certain amount of money out of the sale in order to settle debts or whatever, and that amount could be excessive by your standards.

In Chapter 1 we listed three elements that produce results in small business turnarounds, and the first one was to *find a naive seller.* They do exist. In fact, they are fairly common. Here is one reason: most people who sell a small company do so because they are bored with the business. They want to move on to something else. Almost no one in the world of small businesses really understands how to sell - or buy - a company. That is because these people are experts in their particular field, whether it be selling paper products or manufacturing industrial safety equipment.

You will have numerous opportunities to assess whether or not you are dealing with a naive seller. The very first occurs at your initial contact with the business and its owner. Then there will be more chances to refine your judgment as you get to know the owner better and finally when you get into the due diligence process.

First Impressions and the Naive Seller

People who know what they are doing in the sale of a business prepare a prospectus. So your first hint about the sophistication of the seller is the availability of a prospectus. The uninformed naive seller will know enough, probably, to have the financials for the last three to five years for you, after you sign some kind of confidentiality agreement. If the person doesn't even have the financials on hand, you can bet that this is an individual who hasn't prepared for the sale of the business.

Put yourself in the shoes of the business owner who is trying to sell and wants to do it well. There will be financial information available. But you, as the seller, want to get the best price you can. It's like selling a house. A good real estate agent and smart home owner know that the house has to "show" well in order to sell fast for a good price. No one wants to buy a rundown shabby-looking house. Well the same is true in the buying and selling of businesses. The smart seller will "show" the business as effectively as possible.

How is that done? With the prospectus. That document should include a history of the company, the business lines, the products or services, the marketing and sales methods, and staffing and personnel with particular emphasis on key people. All of that is basic information that needs to be provided in a positive light. "The company has been in business for eleven years. We have three viable business lines that include fourteen products. All of the critical positions in the company are staffed with experienced and competent people." Of course, the document would go into more detail than that.

Here's your first big hint, of course! If there is no prospectus, it hasn't occurred to the owner that "showing" the business is important.

The basics outlined above for a prospectus are just that: basics. A really good prospectus goes one step further. It should discuss the prospects and opportunities for the future. Remember that you are buying the future. The sophisticated seller knows that and helps you understand the potential for continued profitability and growth downstream. If that isn't in the prospectus, then you will have another clue that you are dealing with a naive seller.

The prospectus really should show the re-cast financials, the ones we discussed in Chapter 2. Again, the smart owner knows that valuation will be based on some combination of book value and future cash flow. That same smart owner will lay it out for you. The naive owner won't.

The truly wise seller will give you all of the above and one more item: an updated business plan. If the current owner has taken the time to develop a business plan, you know you are dealing with a pro. And you don't want to use the strategy we are outlining here.

The good business person preparing a company for sale will command a premium because the case has been made in terms of financials and business planning. You don't want to pay a premium. You are looking to buy a business at a discount. Always keep that in mind. Particularly because the good prospectus and business plan will be very persuasive!

Now let's switch from the sublime to the ridiculous for a moment. There is one other clue to a sophisticated seller that should be obvious on your first visit, and that is the physical appearance of the facilities and offices. A fully prepared seller will have made darn sure that the parking area is clean, maybe even newly resurfaced, that the entry way is attractive, that the offices are neat, and that the operations area is well organized. You are looking for just the opposite: a worn down parking area, unattractive entry way, offices crowded with papers and boxes, and a disorganized operations area. Those cues mean two things. First, the business has not be managed very well in the recent past. Second, the seller was not smart enough to realize that the appearance mattered.

Let's summarize the first clues you will get about a naive owner:

- Financials are not readily available or

- Financials are available but there is no prospectus on the business or

- There is a minimal prospectus that describes the history and current status of the business and

- The facilities and offices have not been maintained or improved recently.

On the other hand, the sophisticated buyer will have a complete prospectus, business plan, and a well-run operation.

Meetings with the Owner

You should, after the initial contact, have several meetings with the owner/seller. This is common practice in the selling and buying of businesses. One reason is that some transactions are structured so that the seller continues to work for and with the business for a period of six months to a year in order to assure a smooth transition. Sometimes the seller is retained in a consulting capacity. In either case, it is important that the buyer and seller get along together.

However, one of your principal objectives in these meetings should be to obtain an understanding of the reasons the seller is selling. This may be very straightforward. If the individual is in her late sixties, the most likely reason is retirement, and if she says that is the reason, you usually can believe it. On the other hand, the owner may be in some personal financial difficulties and sees selling the business as a way to generate cash in a hurry. That can be good or bad from your viewpoint. If the seller is really desperate for the money, you might get a quick deal at a discount. If the seller needs a lot of money, however, you could find yourself in a situation where the price is much too high. The seller is asking for what he needs not what the business is worth.

You need to know that one of the most common reasons for selling a small business is boredom on the part of the owner. Anyone who has worked in and particularly owned a small business knows that there is a limit to what you can do to make the work interesting after a period of, say, five years or so. After ten years, there may be a deep need to move on to something else, even if it is another small business in the same area or the same kind of business in another region.

The bored owner can be a boon for you. For one thing, such sellers often are the people who wake up one Monday morning and decide it is time to sell. By Tuesday they are absolutely convinced. On Wednesday and Thursday these folks contact an accountant and lawyer and set the wheels in motion. The astute seller, however, plans well ahead. It can take six months to a year to properly prepare a business for sale, not a week.

Further, the bored owner is motivated to get out and move on and may not be particularly concerned about getting the very best price. In fact, if she or he wanted to get the best price, there would have been more forethought and preparation. Now the same bored owner may be shocked at how low the estimated sale price is. Others will feel that any cash they can generate can be used to move on to another business and will immediately start shopping for the new company to own. That is the best of all worlds for you because it is just like the auto owner who walks into a showroom bored with her old car and ready to buy. Sales people drool over that kind of customer! And you should too.

In talking to the seller, you should be able to get some idea as to how long ago the decision was made to sell and you might even be able to get that person to tell you about preparations for the sale. This often happens when you start swapping stories about businesses you have owned or operated or company owners you have known in the past.

The other kind of information you want to obtain concerns the strengths and weaknesses of the current owner as business person and manager. This will help you in deciding on a business strategy if you do purchase the business, a topic we will cover in a later chapter. But it also gives you clues as to the financial sophistication of the seller. Again remember that you are looking for a financially naive seller. If the owner spends a lot of time talking about operations problems, marketing efforts, staffing issues, and similar matters - avoiding the business planning, strategizing, and financial topics - then you may have the right kind of person with whom to deal.

At some point you will certainly want to ask about the owner's attitude towards business plans and financial projections. The odds are you will get a response something like this: "I understand how important those things are. We do them every once in a while. But I am not really a numbers person. I am not really a structured planner." That's the answer you want to hear.

The reason should be obvious by now. If you are dealing with someone who really understands and enjoys business planning and strategizing, you are also dealing with someone who probably understands the value of the business. That means you will pay a fair price, possibly a premium price for the business. And you want to pay a discounted price for a business that has a reasonable chance of being turned around.

Incidentally, if you are a good conversationalist, most people will eventually reveal their own strong and weak points. They know them. They may be a little reluctant to admit to their weaknesses in a preliminary meeting, but if you start trading stories - and particularly if you talk about your own preferences as a business person - the owner will reveal more than he or she should.

The Desperate Seller

There are businesses whose owners who have to sell. One reason is personal financial difficulty. Whether the owner has gambled away personal money in Las Vegas or is involved in a nasty divorce, there is a need to raise money, usually in a hurry. One way to do this is to sell the business and move on. (Incidentally, there are cases where someone has sold a business in order to keep it away from a spouse who is about to be divorced!)

The advantage in working with a desperate seller is that the motivation to get a deal going is high. The negative aspect is that the seller may need more money out of the deal than you are willing to pay - or should be willing to pay. Or, along the same lines, the seller may need the money faster, in cash upfront, than you can or should provide it.

The other clue to a possibly desperate seller is one whose business has been in Chapter 11 bankruptcy for a while. If the possibility of a self-generated turn-around is starting to look bleak, the owner may be willing to dump the whole thing onto someone else and try again somewhere else at some other time.

There is one factor in dealing with an owner of which you should be aware. It is perfectly all right to ask the owner for his or her personal tax returns for the last three to five years. You can also ask for other personal financial documents such as an estimate of net worth. The owner has no obligation to turn these documents over to you. Someone who has done well with the business or someone who at least has done nothing wrong should be willing to let you see the tax returns. They will be a clue as to how well the individual did personally in owning and running the business. You will also get a clue as to how desperate the seller might be. If she or he is not willing to let you see the tax returns, that could be an indication of a problem. It is a little bit like taking the fifth amendment in a court trial. The act does not automatically mean that the person is guilty but it sure can appear that way.

Due Diligence

Assuming that your preliminary investigation shows promise, the next step in the process is to make a preliminary offer for the business. You stipulate a price, terms, and so on in a non-binding letter of intent. That gives you the right to back out of the deal if it doesn't look good after more study and also provides you with the opportunity to get more details on the business. The latter is known as due diligence. Basically you go in and look at everything germane to the business: accounting and bookkeeping records, tax returns, personnel records, inventory sheets and physical inventory, and on and on. In Chapter 8, we will go over all the elements of due diligence.

At this point you should be using the due diligence process to confirm your initial impression of the business *and of the owner's sophistication or desperation.*

This is not the time to begin making the assessment because you do have some obligation to go through with the deal barring any major discrepancies or problems. You can use the due diligence process to modify your offer, and an modification should be explained based on the information you gathered. For example, you may find that there is a lot of "bad" inventory which would cause you to reduce your offer.

For the purposes of this chapter, due diligence should confirm for you that the owner is somewhat naive financially and may not understand the true value of the business, erring on the side of undervaluing it. Due diligence is discussed in more detail later and is an opportunity to make your final financial analysis of the business, but, again, for the purposes of this chapter, the intent is to confirm your initial impression of the seller.

Preparing to Deal with a Sophisticated Seller

You may not find a business that you understand, that has the right financial and operating situation, *and that has a naive or desperate owner.* Certainly, you won't find that combination very quickly or easily. It will take patience. So you need to know how to prepare yourself to deal with a seller who knows what is going on. This is someone who has made some effort to prepare the business for sale; has retained a good lawyer, accountant, and financial planner; and has made an initial estimate of the value of the business from both a balance sheet and cash flow standpoint.

The key here is to have more information and have performed more analyses than the seller. Information is power, literally and figuratively, in this situation. A truly sophisticated owner will have prepared well for the sale by developing a good prospectus, recasting the financials, showing the estimated cash flow over the next five to ten years, and even providing a business plan that demonstrates how the business can grow over those same time periods. That good owner will have done all this in order to get at least a fair price and possibly a premium price for the business. You need to be prepared to negotiate from a position of strength.

That means two things. First, you need to be able to evaluate the documents you get from the seller very carefully. Your team of accountant, lawyer, and financial planner will become invaluable here. Second, you need to do your own analyses. Don't take the seller's word for anything here. You should do the research to find out the actual total market, how the market is divided up among the competitors, what the likely developments are going to be in products or services, how the business is positioned, and on and on. In other words, you are going to have to work harder and longer in dealing with a sophisticated seller than you would for the naive seller. You can do it. Just remember than it will take more sweat and effort.

■

Chapter 5

ASSESSING YOUR OWN BUSINESS SKILLS AND RESOURCES

One of the keys to making money buying and selling small businesses is to minimize the risks involved and maximize the the probability that you can accomplish the turnaround. There are several possible traps you could fall into, and one of them is buying a business that has problems which don't fit your particular business skills. Your aim should be to acquire a company where your skills will make a big difference in a hurry. Match the business acquisition to you.

There aren't many people with high skill levels in all of the areas needed to operate a small business effectively. In fact, I believe that some of the skills are contradictory. An excellent sales and marketing person often doesn't have great knowledge of finance and accounting - and doesn't want to learn.

In business there is a critical mass, a size at which the business generates enough income to support specialists in operations, finance, marketing, product development, and administration. The problem with small businesses - at least the size we are talking about in this book - is that management usually consists of one person, the owner. There may be some support in one other area from another individual on the team. But the owner/manager is on her own or his own. And therein lies the problem.

In the next chapter, I'll walk you through some of the more common business problems. For example, one of them I have termed "blind management." This is a case where the owner is unable to understand the implications of daily decisions and activities on the financial results of the company. The owner is literally blind to the effects of his or her actions. This usually results from lack of knowledge in bookkeeping, accounting, and finance. As a result, the business is marginally profitable and limping along. If you understand budgeting, cash flow forecasting, and financial statement analysis, you can probably turn such a business around fairly easily. But if your expertise is in marketing and sales with a deficit in the financial arena, then you would be better off steering away from buying such a business.

There are two benefits to an honest self-assessment of your own business skills. First, as I have just pointed out, you can match yourself to the right kind of turnaround situation. The second benefit is that you can incorporate into your business and turnaround plan ways to obtain and use inexpensive outside resources to bolster your skills. You don't have to hire an entire management team or retain several expensive consultants in order to create a full set of business skills and have them applied to your company.

Please note that I deliberately said "an honest assessment" in the preceding paragraph. It's easy to believe that you really do possess all of the knowledge, background, and skills needed to run an entire business effectively. If you do, then you are one of the few "business saints" who has it all. Most of the rest of us have strengths and weaknesses. The best advice I can give is to play to your strengths.

In the sections of this chapter that follow, I will discuss financial and accounting skills, basic business skills, sales and marketing skills, and leadership skills. I will also talk briefly about that most important of all resources: money. And the end of the chapter deals with how to obtain low cost resources to back you up in your efforts to turn around a small business.

Financial and Accounting Skills

To me this is the most important set of skills you can possess as a potential business owner and someone who wants to shape up a business that is having some troubles. Two reasons for this belief. First, these skills permit you to analyze the situation when you are shopping for a business to buy. You will be able to spot the reasons for the problems that plague the business.Second, you have an under-standing of what business activities will affect the "bottom line."

You don't have to be a bookkeeper, accountant, or financial whiz, but you do need to be able to do some basic analyses. At the very least, you should understand the concept of discounted cash flow. If you understand it, the actual computation are not all that difficult on modern hand calculators or with computer spreadsheet software.

Another basic concept is leverage. If working a small business turnaround, you will use a leveraged buy out (LBO in Wall Street terms). That means you will only put some cash down and use borrowed money to finance the purchase. The loan allows you to leverage your cash investment. Be sure you understand the concept of leverage before going into an LBO situation.

Return on investment is also important to you. In buying the small business, you will invest some money. When you sell, you want to get that money back plus some more. The difference or profit you make on the two deals represents your return on investment (ROI). The key here is that your ROI should be equal to or greater than the return on some other investment with equal risk. Your financial planner can assist in this department.

The ability to perform financial statement analysis is vital to valuing the business and then formulating a turnaround strategy. Many books exist on financial statement analysis, and I would suggest that you master at least the fundamentals.

Along with financial statement analysis, you should be able to relate the numbers and ratios to actual operations in the business. For example, one of the ratios used in financial statement analysis is the "turn rate" of inventory. This measures how fast items in inventory are sold. Generally, the faster the "turn" the better the performance of the business. To get a faster turnover, you may need to figure out ways to reduce the inventory and obtain products "just in time" to ship to the customer. The relationship of the way in which product is purchased and held in inventory affects the turnover rate. You should be able to figure that out and do something about it.

Finally, you should be able to understand the effect of standard accounting practices on the financial statements. This was explained, briefly, in Chapter 2. Remember that accountants try to be conservative and use a cost basis for all their work. That influences how the financial statements look. When you make decisions, you should be able to assess the effect of accounting decisions on the cash flow, profitability, and net worth of the business.

Basic Business Skills

These are very basic skills. Some people seem to acquire them almost at birth. Others never quite get there. What are they? Planning, organizing, scheduling, and budgeting. A small business owner who lacks these skills can drive a company into mild to sever problems. Without them, management becomes a continuous "fighting the fire" operation. Whatever crisis occurs next gets the attention. There are no long range plans or even short term ones, for that matter.

If you possess the ability to plan, organize, schedule, and budget, you will bring to many a small company a set of disciplines that can produce a makeover in a fairly short period of time.

However, those kinds of skills are primarily mental. People can have them and still run into trouble because the business world also requires the ability to implement, oversee, and supervise. A plan is fine, but if it does not result in any kind of action, the plan is worthless. So a second set of business skills involves seeing to it that things happen.

There is then a need to evaluate what has happened. The value of a plan is that it permits the manager to assess what has actually happened against what should have happened. Any discrepancy will require corrective action and, maybe, a change in the plan.

In addition to the basic business management skills described in the paragraphs above, there are two more that are extremely valuable to someone who wants to be truly successful in business. The first of these is the ability to negotiate. This requires an understanding of the negotiation process which begins with an assessment of how the other party wants to proceed. There are two styles of bargaining. Positional negotiation is the traditional mode. Each party adopts a position and then they maneuver to see who will change and to what extent. This usually means setting up an initial position and a "line in the sand" position. The idea is that you can give some of the initial position up in bargaining but will not go below the limit case. In most cases of positional negotiation both sides give in a little and move to a common ground.

The second style of negotiation is termed "self interests" method. Here the two sides define what is in their own self interests without establishing a position. Then there is an attempt to brainstorm a solution which will meet the needs of both parties. In positional negotiations, it is common for both parties to feel aggrieved at the end of the process because both have had to give up something. Self interest bargaining tries to avoid that outcome.

You, as a business person, need to be able to engage in both kinds of negotiation and you need to be able to figure out when each type is applicable. Self interest negotiation requires both parties to follow the ground rules.

The other important ability is a willingness to confront other people on matters of conflict or dispute. Some persons find it very difficult to confront another human being. They don't like conflict in any way, shape, or form. The other extreme consists of people who "blow up" regularly. Neither extreme is helpful in the business world.

The ability to confront involves detecting early enough that something is wrong and then approaching the other person in such a way that problem solving can take place. Arguing rarely results in any change. The attacker may feel satisfied but the other person usually become defensive, and defensiveness does not promote change. Effective confrontation means working through the issue or situation that caused the problem and then moving on.

One of the toughest parts of managing a small business: shifting back and forth between the day-to-day details and the "big picture" strategically. Bigger businesses allow the top dog to work on the large scheme of things while underlings get involved in the details. (At least that's the way it's supposed to be!) In your case, you are going to be the upper management team, the middle manage-ment team, and, in some cases, the direct supervisor. Many small business owners agree that it is very difficult to keep the larger perspective in mind when all hell is breaking loose on a daily basis.

Sales and Marketing Skills

It's probably safe to say that a large majority of small businesses suffer from a lack of adequate marketing and sales know-how on the part of the owner. Some owners are good at this part of the business, but typically the small business owner is an expert in a particular field, area, or line of business. For such people the attitude is similar to that of the voice in the movie "The Field of Dreams": build it and they will come. Start the business, offer the product, and they will come. Well, that doesn't happen too often. You have to sell people on the product.

Marketing and sales are really two different but related activities. The first, marketing, is all about getting the word out to people who might be customers. That usually means brochures, product sheets, advertisements, signs, giving talks, and so on and on. No one can or will buy a product unless they know it exists.

The marketing effort also involves an analysis of the competition and how to position the product or service of this company so that it will be purchased instead of the competing products or services. This requires some thought. It also implies that the business owner knows about all of the competition. This part of marketing, incidentally, also gives you clues about how to change the product or service to make it unique in the market place.

Another important aspect of marketing is to conduct customer needs analyses. Too often businesses provide what they think the customer needs.Ask the customers! Find out what bugs them about your product or those of other companies. Ford designed the Taurus by purchasing several examples of each of the competitors' cars in the same price range. Then they had customers drive the autos rating all of the features big and little. Ford then took all of the good features of all the vehicles and designed them into the Taurus. You can do the same with the product or service you provide.

Marketing is only half the story, of course. You need to sell. That means prospecting for customers, finding out where and who they are. It means contacting them on an initial basis. The next step is to show them the benefits of your product or service. And then you close.

Sales is not something that comes naturally to everyone, and there are lots of good sales people who learned their trade. Keep in mind that the most important traits of a good sales person is perseverance. It takes five to seven contacts with a prospect, in most cases, to make a sale.

There are dozens of good books on sales, and every major urban area has sales training courses and seminars. They are well worth the time and money.

Leadership Skills

One of the problems that plagues many small businesses is a lack of leadership on the part of the owner. People who start and operate small businesses are usually experts in some product or service line. They are not trained in the art of leadership. A few get it, maybe through genetics. The rest of us have to learn it.

Leadership is very different from management and from basic business skills. The leader is someone who is able to motivate people without the use of money or other material rewards. Currently, the big word in leadership is "vision." The leader has a vision of what the business could be. But it goes beyond that. The leader is also able to articulate the vision and show people how it can be achieved. It's not enough to just have a dream. At least one foot has to be planted in reality.

There are at least two components to effective leadership. One is a high ability on the professional side whether that be in sales, software development, or fashion design. The other is a concern for employees as human beings. Some people have the great professional skills. That may inspire a few others, but if the highly technical individual cannot relate to people, leadership will suffer. Conversely, there are a lot of nice people who are honestly concerned with others. Unfortunately, many of them are not blessed with a high level of professional skill. They are adequate but not exceptional.

The true leader has to be respected on the professional side and liked on the personal side. Someone who has this combination of abilities is very effective in creating a team effort in a small business, and many small businesses suffer from the lack of team effort.

The Most Important Resource: Money

Probably the most critical skill in buying a small business is the ability to raise money. It doesn't matter how smart you are, how many degrees you have, or how much energy you are willing to expend if you can't raise the money to buy a business in the first place.

There is a standard litany recited whenever someone wants to start a small business and asks where to get the money. That litany also applies to you in your effort to buy a business. The standard list goes something like this, in order of priority and preference:

1. your own savings, borrowing on your home, use of personal credit cards;

2. F&F which stands for family and friends;

3. banks and other lending institutions;

4. suppliers, vendors, and subcontractors;

5. barter and coop arrangements;

6. investment bankers and venture capitalists;

7. stock offerings, private placement or public.

Let's start from the bottom of the list. Trying to obtain equity money by selling stock, either through a private placement or an initial public offering (IPO) is difficult for most small businesses. There are two hurdles. First, it doesn't pay an underwriter to try to get less than $500,000 and a $1,000,000 or more is better. The second thing is that you will get only 50-60% of the money actually paid in. The rest goes to the underwriter, lawyers, and others involved in making sure the offering is legal and legitimate.

The same goes for venture capitalists and investment bankers. They usually don't want to fool around
with small investments. It doesn't pay them to go
through all the paperwork and oversight to invest less
than $500,000. So unless you are shooting for fairly
large businesses by the standards of this book, don't
rely on selling stock or going to a venture capitalist.

That leaves all of the other sources. You need to be
creative in financing your purchase of a small business,
and you need to understand all of the options that are
available. You have to come up with enough dollars to
actually close the deal and, in addition, you will need
money to operate the business and perhaps grow it. If
you put all of your money into the purchase and can't
operate the business, obviously there will be trouble.
And as I have pointed out in another chapter, you need
to be able finance any growth. It is very difficult to do
that by trying to use the cash flow generated by the
business, particularly if the growth is to be fairly rapid.

One technique you should consider is to minimize
the need for cash during operations. Some use of bartering can help here particularly if you have product
or service that other local business people can use.
One case of which I am aware involved a hair stylist
trading haircuts and perms for legal and accounting
advice. (Be sure to understand that this is not a way to
avoid taxes; consult your accountant and attorney to
understand the implications of bartering on taxes.)

Also investigate the possibility of buying some supplies or services on a cooperative basis with other
small businesses. With the advent of large discount
office supply firms, this is no longer as important a

tool. However, if you live some distance from an urban area where these discount suppliers are located, you can coop with other small firms to make a weekly or biweekly run into the city to make purchases. That way at least the transportation costs are minimized.

Suppliers, vendors, and subcontractors can be a source of financing for you. Some large businesses regularly do not pay payables for 60 days or more rather than the conventional 30 days. The additional time allows the business to use its cash more effectively. Of course, that puts a crunch on the smaller business which often cannot afford to alienate the large customer. You do so at your own risk with other small businesses. They may not want to do business with you any more, particularly if you do not warn them in advance of your need to delay payment. Do take the opportunity, however, to negotiate payment terms with vendors and suppliers. They may be willing to allow you to delay payment in some cases or request that you pay a nominal interest rate on the monies owed. You and your accountant need to assess the desirability of such arrangements.

Now comes the issue of dealing with your local bank. Some banks specialize in or at least cooperate with small businesses on loans. They do not lend for any reason to anyone who walks in the door. My banker acquaintances all emphasize the importance of establishing a relationship with the banker before you ask for money. That usually means setting up a checking account and perhaps some kind of interest bearing account before you actually buy a business. Get to know the key persons, usually the vice president who oversees commercial loans. See if she or he is willing to go out to lunch with you. Ask questions about loan policies and requirements.

Once you have a relationship with one or more bankers, you must approach them with a business plan. They will want to know how much money you want, how you intend to use it, how you intend to repay it, and - more importantly to them - how you will secure the note. You can borrow money on receivables and inventory. You can borrow it on real estate or equipment. No bank will lend you all of the amount that is on the books for these items. They typically lend 40-60% of payables, inventory, or fixed assets. The actual amount will depend on their assessment of your business situation.

Some loans are for a fixed period: term loans. Others are more or less continuous, for example, a line of credit. You may obtain a line of credit for which the maximum amount is 50% of your receivables in any given month. That means you have to provide the bank with a listing of receivables at the beginning of each month. You can then borrow up to 50% of that amount.

There are two factors that will determine how easily you can get a bank loan and how favorable the terms are to you. The first of these is the banker's assessment of your business management skills. This is a credibility issue. To what extent can the lender trust your ability to make the business operate with positive cash flow and profitably? Your credibility with the banker is a combination of your personality, how you come across to the bank officer, and of your apparent business skills. A track record really helps. The second part of the assessment is your business plan. To get money from a bank, the business plan has to be solid. It can't be overly optimistic about sales. It should include contingency planning. There should be solid data on market size, sales budgets, operating costs, and so on. Your credibility will be enhanced if your business plan is well written and thought out.

When you develop the business plan and the turnaround plan, one step involves evaluating the average value of the receivable and inventory over the next several months and years so that you can get some idea as to the amount of money you are likely to be able to borrow from a bank. In addition, estimate the amount you could borrow based on fixed assets.

Many if not most small business start-ups are financed by money from family and friends. Instead of the candy M&Ms, you need to think in terms of F&F. How much money can you raise by borrowing from your parents, siblings, aunts and uncles, cousins, grandparents, and anyone else to whom you are related? Maybe you can get a total of $10,000 from those folks in fairly small dribbles. Maybe you can get more. If you have one or two relatives who are fairly well off, perhaps they will put in a sizable amount. (This is one reason to stay on the good side of all your relatives and avoid family fights.)

One of the advantages of borrowing from your family is that it provides great motivation, at least if you are an ethical person. You don't want to see the money your family has put into the business wasted and lost. So you are more likely to work hard and intelligently to get the business turnaround done successfully than if you were using money from some unknown, distant investors.

Of course, you should be honest with these people about the risks involved in investing in your small business turnaround. If you have done your homework, you can be reasonably sure that you will not lose their money even if you cannot provide them with a major return at some future date.

At the top of the list of sources of money are your own finances. I have repeated throughout this book that family and friends, bankers, and outsiders don't want to invest in a situation in which you have no stake. So you have to figure out, with the help of your financial planner, how much cash you can raise on your own before you approach anyone else. This can come from traditional savings. It can result from cashing in retirement plans prematurely even though you will have to pay a penalty and tax on the proceeds. You can borrow on your home equity. And don't overlook credit cards. Five cards with credit limits of $10,000 each represents potential borrowing of $50,000. The cost of that money will be high, but it is available to you.

Finding Low Cost Resources in Your Community

One of the keys to being an effective small business owner is to find and use low cost resources in the community thereby reducing cash flow out of the business. There are, of course, a lot of high priced resources such as management, business, and technical consultants. They charge anywhere from

$50 to $150 an hour, and they may or may not be able to do you any good in efforts to turn around a small business.

Where can you find low cost or no-cost advice and support services? The local Small Business Administration Office is one place. There are numerous publications available at SBA offices. One excellent service that comes through the SBA is SCORE, Service Core of Retired Executives. These are business people, retired obviously, who make themselves available to act as advisors and consultants to small businesses. The services are free. Appendix A lists the Small Business Administration Field Offices where you can get important information on small business management, on SBA loans, and on SCORE services.

The Small Business Administration also has Small Business Development Centers - SBDCs - in many communities. These are usually attached to a local college or university. Their mission is to assist small businesses in their quest for growth and success. An SBDC can provide guidance, advice, and consultation from the staff members or through volunteers who are experienced in small business ownership.

Along the same lines, do not overlook local and state economic development offices. Appendix C lists the state economic development offices. You should contact these folks to discuss your intentions.

Libraries are an important resource for any small business person. Generally you will need access to a library in one of the larger urban areas or at a university. The reference librarian is one of your best friends in the community. That person can assist you in obtaining lists of banks, venture capitalists, business lawyers, accountants, local laws, and similar matters. Libraries are also repositories of information on business data. You can find data on the financial profiles of various kinds of businesses. If the data is not available in hard copy form, many libraries now offer online service capabilities which you can utilize.

When it comes to marketing and business planning, your local library can be of great assistance in providing information on demographics, market sizes, competition, and similar matters. You need to incorporate that kind of data into your planning so that you do not over-estimate the potential market or under-estimate the competition.

Finally, utilize the resources of any local colleges or universities. In some cases, business school classes are looking for situations where they can come in, do their analyses, and make recommendations You may be asked to come to a class and present a particular business problem and let the students and faculty provide input to you. Some schools allow students to perform an independent study project with a particular business. If you can get the right student, that person will be able to do a lot of leg work on the industry, products, markets, and similar issues. Using student resources can be particularly fruitful if the school offers an MBA program when you have access to the more experienced and educated graduate student. University faculty are also available to consult with small businesses. At major universities, these people are expensive because they probably consult with large corporations for high fees. However, at smaller colleges and universities, a faculty member may be pleased and honored to be asked to help you out with a particular business problem. One advantage in using faculty is that they have access to the resources of the university library and university online services which often include the Internet.

One of the best sources of advice and support, once you own a business, is a group of business owners. These exist in many communities and may be organized by the local chamber of commerce, through a community college, or in some other way. The ground rule is that only one business of any one type may be a member. Thus no competitors are in the same group. At meetings, the members discuss common business problems and issues.

You should not overlook the possibility of using small business owners and managers as unofficial and informal advisors. This can be done by taking them out to lunch and just chatting about local business conditions. You will often get good information on who is who and what is what in the community.

Finally, some chambers of commerce can support you in your efforts to buy and turn around a small business. Larger chambers often offer informational and educational programs at no or low cost. Attending their meetings also puts you into contact with local business leaders.

This chapter emphasized the importance of assessing your own business skills realistically. Those were broken down into financial and accounting, basic business, sales and marketing, and leadership skills. No one has all of these skills, so you need to supplement your strengths with people who can provide the information and support in the areas where you are not as strong. In the next chapter, we will review some of the more common problems with small businesses, and in that review, I will point out the kinds of skills needed to overcome each kind of problem. For example, one common difficulty is what I call blind management. This means an owner/manager who does not understand the effect of actions on the financial status of the business. The problem arises because the owner pays no attention to the financial reports issued by the bookkeeper or accountant. In this sense, the manager is flying blind. You need financial skills to operate any business properly.

In addition to skills, you need one basic kind of resource: money. There are various sources of money for your business including yourself, your friends and relatives, banks, suppliers, barter and coop arrangements, and even investment bankers or stock offerings. Every business is short of money all the time, so it is also important to know about and use the low cost or no cost resources in your community.

■

Chapter 6

DIAGNOSING THE TURNAROUND SITUATION

In the previous chapter you had an opportunity to think about and analyze your business skills. The assumption was that no one has all of the requisite skills. That is why most businesses need some kind of management team. One person can't do it all. If a business won't support a full management team, then consultants need to be brought in periodically to provide advice.

To be effective in the turnaround process, you need to match your skills with the requirements of the business, and this chapter is devoted to listing and describing some of the more common ailments in small businesses. There can be an almost infinite variety of problems besetting a particular company, but there are major categories and I believe that ninety percent of all turnaround candidates fall into one or more of the categories presented in this chapter. These most common diagnostic categories are:

- *R.I.P.* - an owner who is Retired in Place.

- *Hobby Shop* - an owner who is having fun while the business is lagging

- *Vampire Ownership* - the current owner is bleeding the company into trouble.

- *Anemia* - lack of capital.

- *Blind Management* - an inability or unwillingness on the part of the owner to control finances

- *Steak with No Sizzle* - a good product or service with inadequate marketing and selling.

- *Unteam* - the business itself is sound but there is a lack of teamwork on the part of employees

- *Senile Product or Service* - the competition has out-run the business line.

- *Wrong place, wrong time* - an improper positioning of the company and its business lines.

Ownership Problems

Three of the most common problems with small businesses are related to the owner/manager. The first of these is *R.I.P., the Retired-in-Place* owner. This situation can come about in many ways but generally is the result of the combination of age and time at the helm, in other words an older owner who has been at the business for twenty years or more. The second most common cause for R.I.P. is a bright owner who has become bored with the business. The challenge is gone.

Large corporations and even some mid-sized companies can afford to have a few people be non-productive and uninvolved, particularly if they are older and near retirement. Even then, these larger businesses tend to provide such folks with an "early out" option or just simply lay them off in this era of right-sizing and downsizing. The small business owner cannot afford to slack off. Yet it happens all the time. And not necessarily to just those over fifty years old. Running a small business is demanding. The business problems are always there. They don't go away on weekends or holidays. These is no one to delegate them to. The owner has to deal with them.

The variety of problems can be staggering. One week it is a production issue in the plant. Then the following week the bookkeeper/accountant gets sick and is out for two weeks. A few weeks later several customers complain. The difficulties are never ending.

No wonder that many small business owners get very tired after seven, ten, or more years. It is very easy to sit back and just not deal with the minor problems. Instead, the manager reads a magazine on industry trend. Soon the small problems don't even come to the owner's attention any more because no one else bothers to deal with them. Then a major issue crops up, and the owner procrastinates on a decision. Finally, three weeks later, the decision gets made, but the precedent has been set: big problems don't need to be handled immediately.

For the next year or two, no one deals with the minor problems and the big ones get handled very slowly. The pattern is obvious to everyone in the company, and the act the same way, ignoring small crises and reacting slowly to big ones. Customers get dissatisfied but no one bothers to find out why. Customer drift away. Equipment begins to wear out, and no one cares. New developments occur in the industry, and there is no one to spur the company on to the challenge.

The business just sort of peters out. That is the result of *R.I.P.*

Clues to *R.I.P.* are fairly obvious. Look for an older owner. Look for an owner who has been running the same business - literally the same size, location, products, and so on - for ten years or more. Look for a run-down facility, older office equipment and furniture. Look for piles of documents laying in the corners of offices because filing has become too much of a chore. Look for employees who are not motivated and don't seem to have much to do. All these are signs of an owner who has quit actively managing the business.

The answer? Often the only thing needed is the energy and discipline of a new manager and owner. For this reason, the *R.I.P.* situation is a good one to take over and turn around. The question that must be answered is whether the place has deteriorated to the point where it can't be turned around, at least not without a large infusion of money and an excess of time and energy. In the extreme, this kind of business results in the *Senile Product* syndrome, and that is a tough one to resurrect.

The second common ownership problem I call the *Hobby Shop.* This is not some one who sells model airplanes, boats, and cars. No, it usually results from a situation where the owner has technical skills that are not matched by her or his business skills. The owner is having fun customizing software or building specialized gunsights for hunters. But the work is so much fun that the work takes longer than originally estimated, yet the owner only charges the original estimate or the advertised price. Consequently there is a low profit margin if any profit at all. The owner is having fun, though!

Engineers, software developers, and technologists in general tend to create hobby shop businesses. This is true for most people with scientific backgrounds. It can happen to market researchers and financial analysts, too. These kinds of people get intrigued with the task. They work for the sake of doing the work and only incidentally to make money.

Some will hire a business manager, but that usually doesn't last too long. The reason is that the business manager tries to instill some business disciplines which only disrupt the fun of the work. So that is the end of the professional manager. And it is back to enjoying the tasks and not worrying too much about the profitability of the enterprise.

You can spot this kind of business, as already suggested, by the fact that the owner is an engineer, scientist, research worker, or simply a tinkerer. Generally these businesses are pretty sloppy and shoddy. Financial records may be minimal. There are diagrams, sketches, flow charts, drawings, pictures, floppy disks, reports, magazines, and books scattered around. All of the organization is in the owner/manager's head.

Be careful about buying a *Hobby Shop* business. Whatever success such a company enjoys is due to the creativity and hard work of the owner. In fact, the business is the owner. In this sense, these businesses are very similar to professional practices. Your dilemma in attempting a turnaround is that the business is built around the owner's expertise and personal contacts. If the owner leaves, there isn't much of the business left. On the other hand, if the owner stays, you will be dealing with someone who is used to being in charge and may be quite resistant to any suggestions or recommendations from the new owner.

Symptoms of a *Hobby Shop* operation are the lack of any kind of plans, schedules, or budgets. There are no goals or objectives. Everything is run by the "seat of the pants" of the owner.

The skills required to turn around a *Hobby Shop* business are basic business disciplines: budgeting, scheduling, marketing, and so on. In that sense these are companies ready-made for a turnaround. But heed the warning above. Putting those disciplines into practice could be very difficult if the prior owner stays around, and if that person leaves, you may not have much left - unless you are able, very quickly, to pick up the technical or professional side of the business and have the industry contacts to continue sales.

The third kind of ownership problem overlaps with the financial issues in the next section of this chapter. This is the situation of *Vampire Ownership*. Here the owner has sucked the business dry in financially. This is very easy to do. Sometimes is happens inadvertently. Sometimes it happens deliberately. The inadvertent *Vampire Ownership* situation occurs when the owner is a pushover for every insurance agent, financial planner, and consultant who comes through the front door. The insurance agent and financial planner sell the owner various plans for taking tax-free or tax-deferred money out of the business. And that is fairly easy to do. The problem is that the business requires some money to operate and grow.

Incidentally, another form of inadvertent vampirism is hiring family members and friends, paying them excessive salaries, and not getting value for money paid. These people just don't help with the basic business problems, but they do get some of the cash the company generates each month.

There are some greedy owners. They see the business as a way to live the good life. And the good life consists of an expensive car, good meals, tickets to local sports events, a large house, a condo in a resort area, and vacations to popular and high priced destinations. The car is a company car. Every meal in a good restaurant is a business meal. The season tickets to the local football and basketball games are company owned and used to entertain customers. The condo may have been purchased as a retreat for company business meetings. The vacations go along with industry conventions in Hawaii. Not hard to see how these kinds of expenses can eat up money that should be going into product development, market development, and hiring better staff.

The signs of *Vampire Ownership*, deliberate or accidental, show up on the financial statements in all of the items I have listed in the paragraphs above. Insurance policies, retirement plans, company cars, season tickets to athletic events, and on and on are sure indicators that the owner is taking a lot of money out of the business, often more than he or she should.

A company suffering from vampirism can be a good candidate for a turnaround. The skills you need are primarily financial. The key is to be able to examine the financials, particularly the existence of owner "perks" on the income statement and perhaps a loan from the business to the owner on the balance sheet.

Financial Problems

Vampire ownership is actually a financial problem brought on by the owner, but consistently the most common financial problem in small business is a lack of capital. I call that *Anemia.* There just isn't enough of the life blood of a business, money, to support all the activities needed to grow the business. If you go to the experts on small business start-ups, they will tell you that lack of capital is the single most frequent reason for new businesses to fail. The business owner has to buy the inventory or materials and the equipment, lease the building or office, and so on, but then come the ongoing monthly cash flow requirements - wages and salaries, insurance premiums, taxes, utility bills, and so on. They have to be paid but there is little or no money coming in for a while. Many new businesses simple run out of money before they can generate enough income to survive.

The same problem dogs the small business owner who tries to grow the company. All or most of the cash goes to paying bills. There is little left over to hire more people, add to the facilities, invest in product or market development. And the owner has no way to raise the money easily, at least so the owner thinks. So the business staggers along at a consistent and slow pace.

Clues to *Anemia* can be found in the financials. The uses of cash are devoted to items which sustain and maintain the business. There is little or no investment in R&D, in market research, or in new equipment or facilities. In talking to the owner you will probably get a sense of frustration about this situation. (Almost all small business owners feel this frustration: "Boy, what I could do if I just had some more money to put into this place!") There may be a business plan which includes ways to grow the company, but the resources are lacking.

What is needed to turn around a business with *Anemia?* Obviously the first requirement is an infusion of money. So you have to have enough money to not only buy the company but also to invest in whatever is needed to make it more profitable and to grow. Along with the money you need the financial and business skills to know where to invest the bucks once you have them. Should they be devoted to an expansion of the product line? To market research? To adding equipment and facilities? To upgrading equipment in order to turn work out more efficiently? Those are the tough decisions that have to be made.

Anemia is a problem that can be solved if you have the resources. Companies suffering from this complaint frequently are healthy in other ways and often are quite well run. The owner simply does not have the ability to obtain more money to put into the operation. The various routes to an infusion of capital are closed off, perhaps by lack of imagination, perhaps by a lack of contacts and opportunities. You can step in as a new owner with the necessary resources and make such a business a true turnaround!

Management Problems

Blind Management exists in some small businesses and is a mix of management and financial problems or, more correctly, a financial problem created by management. It is a common difficulty and results from an inability or unwillingness on the part of the owner to control finances. The reason I call this *Blind Management* is that the owner is blind to the financial issues in the business, in other words, the owner doesn't understand the basic financial situation.

The first and most obvious clue to *Blind Management* is the lack of current financials. If they do exist, the owner has misplaced them. Certainly, the owner has not done any recent analysis of the financials. Even if they are readily available, there probably has not been any attempt to compute the usual ratios - quick ratio, inventory turn, and so forth. For this reason, the owner really does not know what is happening to the company financially.

In this case, you have a ready-made candidate for a turnaround. Why? Because, using your basic business management skills and after reading this book, you <u>will</u> read and analyze the financials. You will know more about the company than the owner. You will know what it is really worth. And you will know where the problems are in terms of operations and administration. The numbers on the income statement and balance sheet will tell you. Assuming that the business is otherwise sound, a company suffering from blind management is always a good candidate for you to take over and turn around.

Another kind of problem is *Steak with No Sizzle.* Small businesses can be divided into two types. In the first, the business is owned and run by someone who understands marketing and sales. The second is one owned and operated by someone who understands the technical side but is weak on marketing and sales. That is a case of *Steak with No Sizzle.* These can be good subjects for a turnaround.

The situation is usually one where there is a basically good product or service but too little attention has been paid to getting the word out to potential customers. Signs that a company is suffering from *Steak without Sizzle* are evident when you ask for sales materials, brochures, mailers, and ads and, particularly, when you ask to see a marketing plan. There isn't one. The owner really doesn't know the size of the potential market, doesn't know his or her market share. The owner hasn't even defined the market or market niche. Sales are based on sending out information or placing ads and hoping that someone will respond.

No problem in defining the skills you need here: marketing and sales. If you are really well versed in this area, the business is a logical one for you to take over. You will probably be able to increase sales volumes and therefore income very easily if not immediately. Even if you are not the world's greatest marketer, you should consider this kind of business for one simple reason: there are literally hundreds of small businesses and consultants in marketing and sales ready to help you. You should be able to get this help fairly inexpensively.

Small business persons often, by the very nature of their personalities, are not good leaders. They are hard working individuals who expect everyone else to be the same. They don't understand why employees are not as dedicated and enthusiastic. If they attempt to motivate people, it is usually through the traditional means: money. That means some kind of bonus or profit sharing system. The result usually is a group of individual rather than a team. I call this *Unteam*.

Modern management theory and research has shown that most people are actually motivated more by a feeling of importance, by work that is meaning-ful, and by input into the process than by just money. In fact money is a substitute for the above. There are numerous examples of people who quit higher paying positions to go where the work is challenging and meaningful or who go to work for themselves at a much reduced income.

You can step into a situation like this and turn it around fairly easily. The trick is to take the *Unteam* and convert it into a team. The clues to a situation where the employees are not a team are often sub-tle, but you can spot them. High rates of absen-teeism, tardiness, and turnover are symptoms of lack of motivation. People who take excessive break times and long lunches exhibit the same lack. A team, on the other hand, consists of enthusiastic people. They come to work on time or early. They hate to miss a day. They wouldn't think of working anywhere else.

The cure for *Unteam* is some leadership. There are hundreds of books and seminars on this topic. If you are going to turn this kind of business around, you will need to understand and be able to put into practice contemporary leadership methods. That usually includes, as a minimum, giving employees a lot of input into their work processes. The idea is that every employee, at least every experienced employee, is an expert is her or his own job. So let them come up with better ways to do things. The pay off is more efficient and higher quality work combined with high morale workers.

Basic Business Problems

Here's a real killer: the *Senile Product or Service.* This is the case where the competition, technology, or the market has outrun the product or service offered by the business. This is the buggy whip company after the automobile has been invented. It is the phonograph record company after audiotape and CDs have been invented. In our modern age, many business lines, products, and services become outdates in a matter of years if not months. As an example, the videotape rental business has probably peaked as of the time this material is being written in 1995. Why? Because movies will be made available on demand via cable or telephone lines or direct broadcast TV before the end of the century. No one will need a VCR. No one will need tapes. The business of renting videotapes will probably survive for a while, but it sure won't be a growing area.

The biggest clue to a *Senile Product or Service* is flat or declining sales. Just look at the gross income for the past three to five years. That should tell you. Then you need to use your common sense. Is this a product or service that anyone will really need in the next five to ten years? What other products or services are taking its place? All you need to do is look around you.

If you were to buy a business in this category, the biggest need is the money and skill to bring the company up to speed, preferably past the competition. This can be difficult. For this reason, I tend to think that a senile product situation is not one you should look into very deeply. Unless you have a really brilliant brainstorm, I wouldn't buy a videotape rental store in the mid-1990s just as I wouldn't have recommended making buggy whips in the early part of the 1900s.

Let me make one small exception to this. There are some products and services that can continue for a long time even though they are not likely to produce much growth. Example? Horseshoe nails. Obviously there was a major drop off in the sale of horseshoe nails when horses were no longer used as the main source of transportation in the world. Railroads, automobiles, trucks, and airplanes replaced the horse-drawn wagon or carriage. But there is still a market for horseshoe nails, and it has, in fact, grown slightly in the last few decades. There has been a resurgence in horse ownership in the U.S. for pleasure, not transportation. The "horsey set" have their horses shoed, and the farrier needs to have horseshoe nails. You have to be pretty clever to see these kinds of opportunities, but they do exist. (I can't resist adding that there is currently a market for horse and cow ointments which seem to be exceptionally effective in providing smooth skin and strong fingernails on humans!)

Also beware of a subset of the senile product or service category, and this is short life cycle business. This is a fairly new phenomenon. I have already alluded to the videotape rental business which was created and peaked in a matter of a little over a decade and now is probably in decline. Any fad business will fall into this category. There was a time when skateboard facilities with ramps, jumps, and curved chutes were popular. Gone now! Again, as I write this, the high-priced espresso coffee shops may be peaking out. It could be that in a few years, there will be many fewer than today.

Some businesses can be ahead of their time - or behind it, examples of the *Wrong Time, Wrong Place* problem. You and I have seen them. A company that is behind the times was covered under the title of a senile product or service. But there are some businesses that are literally ahead of their time. They have a bright idea, but they need to educate customers. On what? Those customers need to be educated on the fact that they need the product or service. That can take time, particularly if there are some traditional, standard ways of doing things that must be unlearned. The current owner probably underestimated the time required and may be limping along. You will need guts to hang in there, and you will need the money to keep on educating the customers. That can be a tough proposition.

A similar situation can exist with the location of a business. Sometimes the owner just flat out picked the wrong location, a common problem with retail operations. I know one owner of a hobby shop who is located a half-block off of a main drag, and no one can really see his sign. Not only that, but a large nearby shopping mall began to crash just as this owner opened his store. Traffic plummeted. Wrong place.

Sometimes the business started out in the right place but shifts in demographics and aging neighborhoods now make it the wrong place. This can be corrected, obviously, by moving the business. The major problem is likely to be the lease on the premises - or ownership of the building and land. That can make it tough to just pick up and move.

Clues to the *Wrong Place or Wrong Time?* Here you have to use your business sense. There aren't going to be any obvious answers in the financials or even in the operation of the business. You will have to dig into the marketing side of the company. Look for situations where there is a large potential customer base but little penetration into that market. Is there a way of doing things now that is "okay" with the customers even though the business has a better way? Look for situations where the customer base is located some distance from the business or where the business is located somewhere that can't be found!

A situation of *Wrong Time, Wrong Place* can be tough to change in a hurry. If it is bad timing, you will need patience plus an infusion of money to educate and inform potential customers. If it is a bad location, you will need to be able to work the change in location in spite of a lease or owned real estate.

Let's summarize the contents of this chapter very briefly. There are good, moderate, and poor bets for turning around small businesses. The best bets are:

- *R.I.P*

- *Vampire Ownership*

- *Steak with No Sizzle*

- *Unteam*

- *Blind Management*

These are good bets because the application of basic business management skills will probably result in a marked improvement in the company in a short period of time. Marketing smarts are needed for a *Steak with No Sizzle* company. And the key to *Unteam* is very effective leadership skills.

A business with a lack of capital - *Anemia* - can be a good turnaround candidate if you have the financial backing to put the dollars into it. I list it here as a moderate candidate because your goal is to buy a business at a low price and sell it high. You really shouldn't have to worry about also putting a lot of money into it for operating capital, to acquire better facilities and equipment, or for continued product development. However, if you do have access to those bucks, then by all means consider a business with anemia. They can be turned around.

There are several poor bets, and these include:

- *Hobby Shop*

- *Senile Product*

- *Wrong Time, Wrong Place*

Each of these can be a candidate but they may take a lot of work or money to make right. The problem with the *Hobby Shop* is the role of the current owner and the odds that the business can be continued without him or her. A *Senile Product* will require an infusion of money for R&D or for the purchase of a product that is more up-to-date. Any business that is in the wrong place or has been created at the wrong time, again, will require an investment of dollars because you will need to move to the right place or else hold on until the product comes into its own. (This assumes that the wrong time means the product is ahead of its time; if it is behind, then you are back into the senile product.)

■

Chapter 7

THE SPECIAL CASE OF BANKRUPTCIES

I noted in an earlier chapter that bankruptcies represent another possible access route to companies which can be turned around. Many businesses operating under Chapter 11 reorganization are viable. They generally have run into trouble because of a lack of money to pay creditors, and that can result from several different situations which are discussed a little later in this chapter.

The Bankruptcy Process

You need to understand the process involved in a Chapter 11 bankruptcy case to deal with such a business, its owner, and its creditors in a sensible way. (For more detailed information on buying bankrupt companies borrow or buy the nice little book by Laurence Kallen, *How to Get Rich Buying Bankrupt Companies,* listed in the bibliography at the end of the book; and be sure to use a business lawyer with competencies in the area of bankruptcy law.) A business owner "declares" bankruptcy by filing a petition with the federal bankruptcy court that has jurisdiction. (All bankruptcies are handled in a federal court.) The creditors of a business can also file an involuntary petition of bankruptcy once they get fed up with the delays in being paid.

The petition of bankruptcy is a one page document. Along with it, the bankrupt company must file a Schedule of Assets and Liabilities and a Statement of Financial Affairs for a Debtor Engaged in Business. Those two forms are standard across the U. S. After filing the schedule and statement, the business is also required to provide the court with monthly updates on its financial affairs. If you go to the court and get access to a bankruptcy case - and they are all available to the public - you need to keep in mind that the schedule and statement represent the condition of the company at the time of filing the petition. That situation could change dramatically in a good direction or bad in the months following the filing.

After the filing, there is a meeting of creditors called by the bankruptcy court. Any creditor can attend that meeting, but according to the experts, most creditors do not show up. There are three categories of creditors: priority, secured, and unsecured. The first two have the highest claims on the assets or future payments in reorganization (more on these categories later). The unsecured creditors, being the lowest on the creditor ladder, can form an Unsecured Creditor Committee to pursue their rights as the case goes along.

The owner of the bankrupt company has the right to submit a plan of reorganization within 120 days of filing the petition. The owner has the sole right to do that in the 120 days. After that, anyone - including the creditors or you - can submit a plan of reorganization to the court. If there is more than one plan proposed, the court decides which one is most beneficial to the creditors and approves that one. Before you get too excited about the 120 days, you should know that the business owner can request extensions of the filing date, and many do just that. However, at some point the court is likely to insist that a plan be submitted. Another key bit of knowledge, according to the experts in this field, is that the creditors can submit a reorganization plan or they can solicit an outsider or outsiders to submit plans.

Once the reorganization plan is submitted and approved by the court, the business continues to operate and pay off the creditors in accordance with their ranking in the hierarchy and the negotiated settlement which is part of the plan. In most cases, the unsecured creditors get only a portion of the monies owed them - "cents on the dollar" is the standard phrase.

During all of the above process and after the reorganization plan is approved by the court, the business continues to operate as usual. The managers are prevented, however, from taking any extraordinary actions that would worsen the financial situation or incur additional debt. Actually, such extraordinary actions can be taken but only with the consent of the court.

Players in a Bankruptcy Case

From the above you can readily see that there is an entire cast of characters involved in a bankruptcy case.

First and foremost, of course, is the debtor, the company in bankruptcy. Then come the creditors. They can include the U. S. government in the form of the IRS, state and local taxing authorities, the bank or other lending agency which has provided the business with working capital or loans for real estate or equipment, any lessors of equipment, vendors and suppliers, employees, employee retirement plans, and anyone else to whom the company owes money.

All of these people have claims on the assets or future earnings of the business. They want to be paid. But there is a pecking order among them which is described below.

Claims on the Debtor and the Reorganization Plan

The plan of reorganization is not a business plan but rather a statement on how the various creditors will be handled. For this reason, you need to know the classes of creditors.

There are four classes of creditors but only three of them are important. The *secured creditors,* as the term implies, are entities or persons who have liens or other calls on the assets of the business through loan agreements or similar instruments. These entities or person have to be paid off first. They are the highest level of creditors.

The next class are *priority creditors,* and this can be a jumble of kinds of entities and agencies. Foremost among them are taxing authorities, particularly the IRS and state income tax units. They have a standing right behind the secured creditors. Also among the priority creditors are any who provided money, goods, or services after the bankruptcy was filed and these would include attorneys, accountants, consultants, and others who help the owner through the process. Also included are vendors, suppliers, and subcontractors who allow the business to continue in operation by providing components, materials, or inventory. Obviously these entities would not make such provisions if they were simply lumped in with the unsecured creditors.

Unsecured creditors are the final and lowest class of creditors. They have no direct call on any of the assets of the business. Because of their lower standing, the bankruptcy laws permit them to band together in a committee of unsecured creditors.

There are, finally, the *shareholders* in the corporation or *partners* in the partnership. The balance sheet will generally show a zero or minus owner's equity. That is the risk these people take in investing in the business, and the bankruptcy laws do not protect them. In effect, shareholders take on the normal risks of business success or failure in return for being shielded from the debts of the corporation.

In order to buy a business in bankruptcy, you will have to submit a *plan of reorganization,* and that plan will classify all of the claims against the company. After they are classified - supplier Bill is an unsecured creditor, banker Jane is a secured creditor, the state income tax office is a priority creditor - the plan must show how each class will be treated. For example, the secured creditors will be paid in full but the terms of repayment will stretch out the time period by an additional two years. Priority creditors will be paid $0.90 on the dollar, also stretched out. And the unsecured creditors will be given $0.15 on the dollar over the next three years and will be given one share of stock in the company for each dollar owed.

This is all well and good but the bankruptcy court and creditors want to see something else in the plan of reorganization: where will the money come from? A plan that suggests everything will be paid out of cash flow - when a cash shortage caused the bankruptcy - is not likely to be accepted. You will need to show that there will be an infusion of cash or that some assets will be sold or some other means used to generate the funds needed to pay of the creditors. Of course, if the unsecured creditors are given stock, that settles that, but the plan will have to show how they will have rights through voting stock and perhaps representation on the Board of Directors.

Once the plan of reorganization has been generated, a disclosure statement is sent to all the active parties 25 days prior to a hearing before the judge. All of the creditors have to vote favorably on the plan and then the judge must approve it. If there is more than one plan and several are voted on by the creditors, the judge gets to decide which plan is most favorable *to the creditors*.

There is one other item you need to know. If one class or group of creditors do not vote favorably on the plan but everyone else does, the judge can cram the plan down on the resistant creditors. That is called, in bankruptcy jargon and quite accurately, a "cramdown."

Assessing the Business Situation

The big question, of course, is: what caused the bankruptcy? Filing for bankruptcy is a final and major step for most small businesses. That means things have been going bad for a while. Something is wrong. A clear-headed assessment of the problem is very important for you as an investor.

Most bankruptcies occur when the business can no longer pay all of its bills. That means a shortage of cash. Of the illnesses described earlier in this book, anemia and vampire ownership are likely causes. A lack of operating capital - cash - eventually can create a situation where the business cannot meet its obligations. And an owner who is sucking money out like crazy in order to finance her or his own activities will create a similar situation. The cure is capital, and if you have the dollars to invest in an otherwise sound business, you may be able to salvage this kind of situation.

There is one "good" cause of bankruptcies, and it would fall under the category of blind management, an owner who didn't keep track of expenses and cash flow. That specific situation is one of rapid growth. Many small business persons don't realize how much money is needed to grow a business. Back to financial basics. If you start a business, you will have to spend some money before any income is generated. The same holds true in growth. The owner will have to buy goods, materials, inventory, components, or whatever in order to sell more. That takes money. The owner will have to hire more sales people or operations personnel to handle the added work. That requires paying wages. The money will have to be paid before the added income materializes, before the checks arrive from the customers. Sometimes it takes months, maybe even a year or more, for the sales levels to increase significantly. Somewhere along the line, the business runs out of cash. Success can spoil the party.

If you run into a situation where the business was growing and outgrew the financial resources of the owner, you have run into a good situation. This is one you might be able to salvage fairly easily. At least you know that the product or service was good and the marketing effective. Your task will be to improve the financial smarts of the company.

Sometimes a business owner can be guilty of making one bad decision that creates the eventual need to file for bankruptcy. One company calls these "waterline" decisions. If the decision is a bad one, the damage is below the figurative waterline of the business and it will begin to leak. This can happen in a business that in all other respects is solid. That, again, is a good situation for you to look at carefully.

The final reason for bankruptcy that I will point out here is simply bad luck. Most often this occurs when a major customer cuts back on its business. The resulting loss of revenue to the small business is enough to create a major problem, particularly if management could not cut back on expenses fast enough.

If the big business not only cuts back but goes belly up, the reduction in income is bad enough, but the small business is now an unsecured creditor to a larger business that is in bankruptcy. The invoices submitted so hopefully over the last few months are now worth cents on the dollar - if anything at all.

How to Proceed with an Offer

Your first step should have been to review the papers filed in bankruptcy court, the bankruptcy petition and schedules. That will permit you to do a preliminary screening. Suppose that you find a likely candidate for your purposes.

Next you approach the owner. This is tricky. The owner is someone who has been through hell for the last months, maybe a year or more. That person is likely to be wary and defensive. Creditors have been beating on his door. He is trying to run the business while meeting with lawyers and accountants.

The experts in this field advise that you approach the owner as an investor rather than as a potential buyer, that is, unless you know for sure through prior knowledge that she or he is ready to sell. Come in like a white knight to rescue the owner. Discuss the situation. Find out what the owner is feeling. Find out what has happened and what is likely to happen in the bankruptcy process.

Eventually, you may want to suggest to the owner that it would be easier if you simply bought the company. That may take a great load off of the owner. Your offer may be welcomed. On the other hand, the owner may see years of hard work going down the drain, and you will be ushered out of the building.

You can then approach the creditors. Particularly the banker or other major lender. These people are likely to want to see the situation remedied, and the sooner the better. Again, you may have to go slow and build a relationship with the loan officer. Although she wants to get the risky business situation cleared up, she also wants to make sure that she does not create a problem while trying to solve one.

If you work through the creditors - secured, priority, and unsecured - you will be attempting a hostile purchase, at least hostile to the current owner. The creditors can be convinced that you are on the up and up, and that you offer a better deal than the owner can produce. Then you have a chance of buying the business through a plan of reorganization.

So that is your final step. Develop a plan of reorganization with your accountant, lawyer, and financial planner. Be wise and work out a business plan for the turnaround as discussed in Chapter 12 as well. Having a well-documented plan will make the creditors even happier and you more credible.

If the owner is amenable to a sale, then you will need to deal with that individual and at the same time develop the plan of reorganization because the creditors - and court - will want to know what the sale of the business means in terms of paying off debts.

And a final note of caution. If a bankrupt company, a Chapter 11 case, looks appealing to you, be sure that your attorney understands all the ramifications of bankruptcy law. If not, then retain one who does. This can be a minefield if you're not careful.

■

Chapter 8

DUE DILIGENCE

Buyer beware! Old advice to consumers that applies to you as a purchaser of a business as well. The advice is put into practice in something called "due diligence." This is where you take a careful look at the business to make sure that what is represented on paper actually exists.

Financial Due Diligence

Working our way down the typical balance sheet, start with cash and cash equivalents. If they are going to be part of the deal, you need to verify the bank balances and statements from brokers or other organizations where the business has investments. This is usually fairly straightforward.

Next come receivables. If there are a lot of small receivables, you will want to spot check much as an auditor would do. Pick fifteen or twenty invoices at random and verify that they have in fact been sent out to customers. Very important in this part of the due diligence process is to obtain an aged receivables list from the bookkeeper or accountant. As you know, this shows how long the various receivables have been out to customers, and your objectives is to assess how "good" the receivables are. If all of the receivables are for less than thirty days, there is no problem. The customers pay on time. On the other hand, if twenty percent of the receivables are over 90 days old, a problem exists. Either the business is not very aggressive in pursuing collections or the customers are facing some kind of financial difficulty, maybe a local, regional, or national downturn in the economy. This should be a warning flag to you.

The next step is to ask about collections policy. Have letters been sent out to customers with overdue accounts? How many and at what intervals? Have any accounts been turned over to a collections agency? Ask for documentation and try to understand how the situation arose.

The second part of this analysis of receivables is that it permits you to re-value the net worth of the business. Receivables are assets. If some of them are not recoverable, the total dollar value of the assets is reduced. Your best bet would be to take the list of aged receivables and apply some kind of adjustment based on your own common sense and business judgment. For example, you might take the receivables under 30 days at 100% of value but reduce those between 30 and 60 days to 95%. Then discount the much older receivables, those between 60 and 90 days to 80% of their apparent value and eliminate any receivables over 90 days as probably uncollectable. Or you might reduce those older receivables to 25% of their apparent value.

The next item on the balance sheet is usually inventory or work in process. A concern here is that the inventory shown on the books actually exists in the back of the store or in a warehouse somewhere. This means you have to go look! You don't take someone's word, and, in fact, it is wise to open some boxes and see what is inside. A small percentage of business owners, the sleazy ones, have been known to keep boxes of bricks and pawn them off on auditors and potential buyers as cans of paint or computer printers or books.

Work in process is used in manufacturing operations. Such businesses often have an inventory of parts and components and another inventory of completed products. But in between there usually are some partially completed products. This may also consist of subassemblies in which parts have been put together but not yet into a complete product. Work in process includes not only the value of the components but also the labor required to do the assembly.

Here again you need to go out on the shop floor and verify what actually exists. A good accounting system will track work in process, but it could be that the bookkeeper did not subtract the value of goods as they went out the door resulting in a work in process number that far exceeds what is actually on the factory floor. For that reason you need to take the accountant's version of work in process and check it against the physical objects in the plants.

Moving on, due diligence should also cover fixed assets such as equipment, machinery, real estate, and buildings. These are usually fairly easy to verify, but you do need to look over the related documents such as bills of sale, deeds, and so on. You want to make darn sure that the owner of the business really owns the fixed assets.

The final part of the usual balance sheet asset list is concerned with notes. If someone owes money to the business, check to see that the note is in order and that payments have been made in a timely fashion. This is like receivables, and if the individual or business owing the money has not paid according to the terms, the note may not be worth its face value.

There often is a small item on the balance sheet called prepaid expenses. If this is small there is no sense in spending a lot of time checking it out. But if the dollar value is fairly significant, you might want to find out what expenses were prepaid and obtain evidence that the payments were, in fact, made.

Now you go through the liabilities in the same way. How current are payables? If they aren't current, why? And are there any penalties that might have to be paid?

A critical item here, by the way, concerns payroll taxes. If the business is behind on these, there is a major potential problem with the IRS, and you don't want to buy that problem!

In the liabilities area, you also want to look into any notes the company owes to individuals or other business entities. Make sure the terms of the notes have been met to date and that you can live with them.

A brief caution is appropriate here before moving on to a discussion of the income statement items. In an asset sale (described in Chapter 11), the seller makes legal representations about all of the assets. Your lawyer will point this out to you and be of great assistance in drawing up the sale documents. These legal representations, for example, will state that the inventory consists of a certain number of a specific kind of product. If that turns out to be false, the seller is liable because she or he signed the representation and will owe you some money. The problem is that you may have to go to court to get that money and pay legal fees along the way. It's better to perform a thorough due diligence before making a deal than trying to recoup some money after closing.

Now let's move on to the income statement. The first item there is gross sales. Most businesses are operated on an accrual accounting basis which means that a sale is recorded when an order is received from a customer. (In a cash system, the sale is recorded when the customer's check arrives.) You need to verify that there really are purchase orders or contracts to match the sales figure shown on the P&L. Again, most small business owners are honest, but a few try to pull tricks. One of those is to count a "sale" after a customer has been contacted and promised to buy something but before a purchase order is in hand. Another one is to count merchandise that has been put out on consignment as sold.

The remainder of your due diligence on the income statement will probably be related to the accounting system. A concern here is how costs are allocated. A good cost accounting system will be of great help to you because it will show sales by category of product or service, costs in 'the same way, and the contribution to overall profitability for each product or service type. You may need the help of an accountant in reviewing the accounting system and the validity of its reports.

Based on the advice I provided in Chapter 2, you also need to look closely at the fixed expenses on the income statement. This is where owner perks usually appear in the form of a company car, key man life insurance, or a retirement plan. These are the items you will add up to find the total cash flow that would be available to run the business assuming that you do not take advantage of the same perks. Again a reminder! Your objective is to increase the value of the business and sell it at a higher price, and it is not to drain money out of the business as you run it.

You also need to be alert to any unusual items on the P&L. For example, there may be a very large contribution to income from non-operating assets. This happens when money is coming in from notes or investments in other businesses. (It can also happen if the business is into money-laundering, but we will assume that you won't be looking at that kind of business!). Again, use your own business judgment and the advice of your accountant and attorney on these matters.

Reworking the Balance Sheet and Income Statement

Having gone through due diligence, it is now time to take another look at the financial statements and to rework them one more time. Adjust the assets in accordance with the results of the due diligence effort. Do the same for liabilities. The result will be a new net worth number for the business which may be higher or lower than the one on the owner's balance sheet.

Take the income statement and pull out all of the owner perks or other drains on cash flow that you believe could be eliminated when you take over. This represents the cash flow that you can obtain from the business. Your next step is to create a business plan to increase sales, decrease cost of goods sold, and decrease fixed expenses. This is explained in Chapter 10.

Agreements, Contracts, and Leases

You have taken care of the financial due diligence if you went through the process described in the preceding paragraphs. Your job is not done.

All businesses are involved in agreements, contracts, and leases. There are several key issues to consider here. First you should make sure that the agreements, contracts, and leases are transferable. Some are. Some aren't. If they aren't, you will have to re-negotiate them. For example, some building leases specifically state that they will be re-negotiated if transferred to another party.

Take the time to read - or have your attorney scan - all of the agreements, contracts, and leases. You may find some pleasant or unpleasant surprises. There could be favorable terms to some of these items which makes them valuable to you. One business found that the lease on its building was for 25 years with no inflation escalation clause! A good deal. There can be negative stipulations as well. An office equipment lease may have an onerous provision requiring purchase of the equipment at an unknown to-be-determined price in three years.

You should also be looking for contingent liabilities in this area of your due diligence. When you go through the files, are there potential lawsuits? Is there an unfunded pension liability? (Yes, that happens in small companies as well as large.) Is there a pending workers compensation case? Look carefully at all of the paperwork in the company's files.

Physical Facilities and Equipment

There is one big obvious key item here: hazardous waste and environmental clean-up. You certainly don't want to buy a business in which there has been improper disposal of hazardous materials. The problem here is that the hazard may not have been created by the current owner, and he or she may be unaware of it. But it will pass on to you if the business created the mess in the past.

Look around the building and grounds. Look for oily, greasy areas. Look for five gallon drums stored in a fenced-off area. Ask what they are. Ask to look inside or have an expert check them.

You should also inspect all of the major items of equipment that go along with the business to make sure that they have been well maintained and are currently operable. How clean is the equipment? Are there inspection and maintenance records? Are they up to date?

The same goes for the building and grounds. Look for evidence of water leaks in the ceiling and on the walls. How old is the roof? How recently has the building been painted? What is the condition of the parking lot? Is there a security system? And on and on.

Key Personnel

My own business philosophy is that people really are the key to a successful enterprise. As a potential buyer you need to spend some time assessing the personnel who make up the business team. There are two sides to this coin. Some small businesses have one, two, or more key individuals who have kept the whole thing afloat, sometimes in spite of the owner/manager. You need to try to figure out who these people are. Conversely, there may be one, two, or more people who have been deadweights but managed to survive because the current owner didn't have the courage or insight to get rid of them. Clearly, you want to keep the key contributors and be prepared to replace the others. That last comment is important. You can't just fire them. You have to figure out a way to replace them with someone better. Or in this modern era of downsizing and rightsizing and re-engineering, you need to figure out how to maintain the productive output of the business while eliminating those positions.

A word of caution here. "Key" does not always mean supervisory or management personnel. Many small businesses have skilled employees at the working level. They know more about the product or service than the managers because they have dealt with it for years. Similarly, a trusted bookkeeper may understand the finances of the business better than the current owner. Your task is to try to figure out who is really "key" and who isn't.

Part of your due diligence process should be a short interview with each of the key personnel in the business. This is a touchy part of the due diligence process and may not even be possible in some cases. If the owner has informed her or his personnel of a possible impending sale, then there is no reason why you should not have access to those people. On the other hand, if the owner has kept quiet and not told the staff, there is no way you can appear and interview them as a potential buyer. *However,* you can make a suggestion to the owner. It may be possible for you to show up and do the interviews as a management consultant retained by the owner. This would permit you to ask pertinent questions about the operation without tipping your hand or that of the owner. The problem with this strategy is that, if you complete the deal, the employees are going to have some questions about how and why you were able to interview them without saying anything about the acquisition. (I also need to add here that I would be leery of a situation in which the seller is reluctant to announce his or her intention to sell.)

Assuming that you are able to meet with the employees, what should you ask? First and foremost, use open-ended questions. What do you do? How do you do it? Why is it done that way? Do you have ideas on how things could be done more effectively or efficiently? What kind of background do you have in this work? Where else have you worked? What are your plans for the future? This is a combination of a standard employment interview and a consultant's search for problems and solutions.

Your Final Offer or Retreat

You will modify your initial offer based on the result of the due diligence process and the business plan you develop from the re-worked financials. Here is what frequently happens. Analysis of the balance sheet will reduce the assets by some amount because of adjustments in receivables and inventory or work in process. However, there may be offsetting adjustments resulting from hidden assets. Your analysis of the income statement may show that the business has the potential to throw off sizable cash flow. Now remember that you are really buying the future cash flow of an operating business and, unless there are a lot of good fixed assets, you aren't buying the assets minus liabilities, the book value of the company. The owner will see the book value as the worth of the company.

Having done due diligence, you have several options. You can *proceed* with your original offer. This would occur if the profitability and cash flow look good and there were not too many large adjustments to assets. You can *increase* your original offer. This would happen if things really looked good and you wanted to close the deal quickly by making the owner a better offer. Or you can *decrease* your original offer. Why? Because the cash flow doesn't look all that good, and you made some significant adjustments to the book value which reduced it. The hazard in a reduced offer, obviously, is that the owner won't like it. He or she was counting on at least the original offer and maybe hoping to negotiate you into a higher number. Now you come back with a lower price. That could result in "no deal." Of course, if it isn't such a good deal anyway, who cares?

Some other possibilities exist. You may want to modify the terms of your offer other than or in additional to the price. For example, you may want to exclude certain assets or liabilities. After due diligence, your business sense tells you that these assets or liabilities will do you no good and perhaps be a drag on the business. You can specify such changes to the agreement in your final offer.

The last option is to withdraw your offer based on the due diligence findings and business planning. *Always keep this as an option in your own mind.* It is very easy to become captivated and fascinated by the business after a detailed look into it, after interviewing people, after fantasizing about what you could do to shape it up. This is like driving a new car out of the showroom for a test drive. Sales people know you are more likely to buy once you have been seated in the car, turned on the ignition, moved down the street, and listened to the stereo. Same goes for buying a business. The more you get into it, the more likely you are to want to buy. Discipline yourself! Use your advisors! No matter how much you think you could turn around the company, be hard-nosed and look at the numbers. Again: you are investor looking for a pay off. Keep that attitude in mind as you complete due diligence. Here's the key question: if a stock broker offered you shares in the company at the price you are offering, would you buy the stock? If your answer is yes, then proceed. If not, back out. Go on to another likely prospect.

■

Chapter 9

ASSESSING RISKS

A smart business owner always looks at the risks in a business venture, and you need to do the same, particularly in attempting to turn around a company that may have some problems. There are six kinds of risks to consider.

Turnaround Risks

This is, of course, your main concern. You are betting on your ability to increase sales and cash flow, to improve the balance sheet net worth, or to show a potential next-buyer the true worth of the business. Some turnarounds are relatively easy. Some difficult. In Chapter 6 on diagnosing turnaround situations, I tried to give you some basis for evaluating the potential for improving businesses based on the problems that have plagued them in the past.

You should look over the financial statements very carefully and perform the kinds of analyses discussed earlier. You should talk to the current owner at length. You should talk to the key personnel in the business. You should do the due diligence described in Chapter 8.

After all of that, you ought to have a pretty good picture of the business, where it stands, and where it might go.

What else can you do? Go and get some outside opinions. An experienced business lawyer, one who has dealt with a number of business acquisitions, can frequently give an opinion. Similarly, an accountant who understands business operations can provide valuable input.

Go beyond those folks. Retain a business consultant. Maybe two. Have them look over your assessments, the financials, and your business plan and turnaround plan, and then ask them for an honest opinion as to the feasibility of what you are trying to do. Let them advise you on the realism of your time table and your financial projections. These are people who have no stake in the transfer of the business from the current owner to you. They won't make an extra nickel if you buy or if you don't buy. And that makes their opinions important.

The reason for going to these lengths is that the longer you look at, analyze, talk, and plan, the more you will get emotionally involved in the business. It may begin to look better and better to you. This is particularly true if you have been searching for a while and want to get on with the program. After a while, any business can begin to look good. It's kind of like a lonely single hungering for a partner. Any live breathing candidate becomes acceptable. Go slow. Stand back and take a careful second and third look. Get outside opinions.

Normal Business Risks

Every business faces some risks - fire, flood, wind, robbery, injury - which can be handled through insurance plus astute managing. Fires, accidental and set, represent a major problem particularly for restaurants, furniture finishing operations, gas stations, and other places where flammable materials or flame are part of the business. Natural causes and disasters can wreak havoc on a business, its facilities and equipment. Every year tornadoes, hurricanes severe thunderstorms, floods, lightning and high winds cause millions of dollars in damage. There is always the possibility of some really unusual accidents: a drunken driver plows through the front window of a store or part of an airplane falls through the roof of a factory. There is always the possibility of theft, pilfering, or embezzlement. In the retail trade, shoplifting represents a continuing and real threat. Many or most of the events described here can be covered by appropriate insurance, and you should make sure that your acquisition is properly protected - but at a reasonable price.

Workers' compensation plans exist to assure make sure that employee injuries can be handled without creating a serious financial drain on the business. There is also the possibility of a customer or supplier being injured - maybe slipping on an icy sidewalk or tripping on a worn carpet - and suing you and your company. That's what insurance is for!

Don't overlook the possibility, a very real one, that you or an employee could be involved in an automobile accident while performing job-related duties. That is particularly relevant if a company car is involved. In either case, the company can be sued for the injuries and damages suffered by the other party.

The other kind of disaster that can strike is loss of data now that computers are used in virtually every business. A power outage, lightning strike, or voltage surge can create havoc with computer memories. Insurance can cover some of this kind of loss, but the use of surge protectors and backup power sources is mandatory.

In addition to insurance, you should make sure that there are adequate security measures, safety programs, fire prevention methods, and employee training efforts to minimize the risks.

Competitive Market Risks

Every business - well almost every business - faces competitive market risks. There are other people out there trying to sell their products and services to the same people you are targeting. Some of these other business are direct competitors. They sell the same stuff you do. Maybe they sell it cheaper or provide better service. Maybe their product or service is better - or worse - than yours. That is part of the business of business.

These risks can be reduced by being good at what you do. If you provide better service at a lower cost with a superior product, you will get more sales and make more money. That is the challenge you face. It's not enough just to provide better service if your price is too high. It's not enough to sell at a lower price if your customer service is lousy or your product doesn't meet customer needs. It's not enough to have the best product available if you have to sell at a very high price and ignore the customer after the sale. You have to do all three at once. Chances are that the business you are buying dropped the ball on one, two, or all three of those counts. Now it is up to you to shape up the company to be competitive. So you can minimize that kind of market risk.

Something else can happen. Customer desires, needs, and wants can change. This is particularly true in areas where fads and fashions dictate sales. As I write this, micro-breweries and cappuccino coffee houses are popular. How long will that fashion last? I can't predict. By the time you buy and read this book, one or both may be history. Chocolate chip cookie stores in malls seem to have disappeared in the recent past, again as I am writing. So you need to be careful in assessing the odds that the product or service is something that people will continue to seek out.

Economic Risks

Economics is called the dismal science. It can be really dismal if the economy turns against you. The major risk, of course, is a downturn in the economy. Such a recession, mild or severe, crimps the ability of customers to buy. They pull in their horns, cut budgets, and spend less.

The best way to guard against this kind of economic risk is to run your business in such a way that you can cut back your expenses and ride out the downturn. That may mean using contract and temporary employees. It may mean subcontracting some parts of the business operations to outsiders. It definitely implies not getting overly invested in expensive equipment that needs to be operated at near capacity in order to pay off the debt taken on to buy it. Here the skills of the prudent business person are vital.

In the past there has been a danger of large shifts in interest rates. The volatility of interest rates seems to have lessened since the early 1980's. However, there is still some range of variation that is inevitable as the Federal Reserve and Treasury attempt to control inflation. The best safeguard against large changes in interest rates is to minimize borrowing. That doesn't mean no loans at all, but it does mean small short-term borrowing so that you can take advantage of downward drift in interest rates and minimize borrowing if interest rates head up.

The story is somewhat similar with regard to inflation. Our economy seems to be fairly well regulated at this time. Inflation is all in your favor if you have bought a business and then want to sell it because the fair market value of assets will probably have risen. The opposite is also true. If you bought as inflation was moving prices up and then the economy became stagnant and inflation rates dropped - or there even was a case of deflation - your investment will have decreased. This does not appear to be a serious risk just as the possibility of benefiting from high inflation isn't too reasonable. Protection from inflation risk is based on your ability to estimate the likely trend over the period of time you will own the business.

R&D Risks

There is always the possibility that someone will develop a product or service that greatly improves on what you are doing. Your business can literally be made obsolete. As I am writing this chapter, the travel agency business is experiencing serious difficulties. One reason, among several, is that the air lines are formulating plans to allow "ticketless" travel. Someone wanting to fly from Pittsburgh to Chicago would simply call a reservations clerk - or maybe even bring up the right screen on a computer - and select a flight and seat. Payment would be made by credit card or electronic transfer. There would be no need for a ticket, just a code number. Our traveler would show up at the airport where an agent would check the computer reservations system, ask for picture identification, and provide a boarding pass. No need for a travel agent!

Reducing R&D risk can be done in two ways. The first is to select a business that seems impervious to rapid change. One that comes to mind is the garden supply business. Another is pet care. You need to recognize that trying to pick a business area that is not likely to change is risky.

The more sensible tactic is to engage in R&D yourself or, at least, to stay abreast of the changes that are occurring in your line of business. The ideal situation is to be ahead of the pack in developing new and better ways to serve your customer. We need to include here not only new products and services but improved ways of delivering them and ways of reducing costs and prices. People who are good at this game are not necessarily brilliant engineers, scientists, or innovators but rather simply in touch with their customers and what those customers want and need. Sometimes the customer doesn't know exactly what she or he needs, but you can watch how, where, when, and why they use your product. Improvements may become immediately obvious that you wouldn't see sitting in your office or wandering around the shop.

■

Chapter 10

EXIT AND BUSINESS PLANNING

Remember you are a sophisticated buyer - hopefully dealing with a naive seller. Part of your sophistication is the ability to do exit and business planning. Let's take them in order. Both are important.

Exit Planning

All business owners should have an exit plan but few do. The exit plan specifies what you want to get out of the business when it is sold. Not "if" it is sold, but when. You are buying this company in order to improve its situation and then re-sell it for a profit.

An exit plan is not complicated, certainly less complicated than a business plan. There are three key elements to the exit plan: in how many years do you want out? how much money do you want and under what terms? and what will be your relationship to the business after you leave?

Someone who already owns a company may set a time span anywhere from a year ahead to ten or fif-

teen years from the present to get out. Your preliminary assessment of the business you intend to buy will
provide a guideline for how soon you can move on.
There are some exceptional - and very lucrative deals
- that would permit you to exit with a year or two of
purchase at a handsome profit. More commonly you
will have to stay around for a period of three to five
years to make the turnaround work. The length of
time will depend on the kind of business, its current
status and future outlook, and the amount of time and
money needed to make it salable at a profit to you. In
this area the exit plan and business plan are linked.
The business plan will give you a clue as to how soon
you can expect to put the place back on the market
and sell it.

The second major issue is how much money you,
as the business owner, expect to get out of the business and under what terms. As I have stressed several
times, most naive owners want at least the apparent
book value of the company where that apparent book
value is what the balance sheet says today. Some owners will want a premium over that amount. You will
not be a naive owner and should have solid numbers
to back up your expected selling price.

While the selling price is a magic number to most
business owners, the astute know that the way the
deal is structured is just as important. The price paid
by the buyer most commonly consists of a cash payment, a note carried back by the owner, and a salary
or consulting retainer to be paid to the owner for a
fixed period of time. As an example, a buyer may
want to provide the seller with $50,000 in cash, obtain

a note for $100,000 from the seller to paid over a period of five years, and pay the seller a consulting retainer of $25,000 a year for two years. The total is $200,000. Of course, the seller has to calculate the discounted cash flow because some of the money, actually a good part of it, will be coming in years ahead. The current owner would be much better off with a cash deal for $200,000.

The important point to keep in mind is that the purchase of a business usually involves a cash payment, a carryback note by the seller, and some kind of retainer or salary for a period of time.

Finally, there is the issue of how you as the seller will relate to the business in the future. A certainty is that the buyer will want a "non-compete" agreement. She or he will not want you to start or buy another business of the same type and become a competitor on her or his money!

Sales agreements usually involve some kind of transition period during which the current owner assists the new owner in maintaining and growing the business. A period of three to six months is usually appropriate for this purpose. In that space of time, the former owner may be retained as a consultant or put on the payroll as a part- or full-time employee. There are some situations, however, where the seller leaves the company on the day of closing never to darken its door again. That is unusual.

For some business owners the exit plan decisions can be complex. For you, they are simple. Because you are in the business of turning the business around for the purpose of making a profit, you should try to get as much cash out of the deal as you can upfront - because you want to go on and do another deal. A long term payout is not worth your while. You don't want to end up working for the new owner or owners for an extended period of time. You may have to give them six months for an orderly transition. A traditional small business owner might want to hang around for a year or two. Not you.

The exit plan and business plan or turnaround plan overlap in one area. Your exit plan should include the time frame you anticipate for the turn-around and that is predicated on what the business plan says is feasible. You may find that the business plan suggests the business can be turned around in two years and you add on another year or two to effect a sale. So your exit plan says that you want to be out of the business as an active agent in three to four years.

The business plan suggests that you can increase the value of the company by forty percent in the two year period. It appears that the purchase price to you will require an investment of $50,000 in cash and that the total price will be $150,000 with $100,000 in a carryback note to the present owner. The forty percent increase means that you should be able to sell the company for $210,000. You will pay off the remainder of the note to the previous owner, say $90,000 and see $120,000 pretax proceeds for a gain of $70,000. So your exit plan states that you want your $50,000 initial investment back plus another $50,000 in cash. The remainder can be a note secured by the assets of the business.

In this example, the exit plan is worded as follows: "I want to spend no more than four years in improving the sales and profitability of this company so that it's value is increased 40%, and I want to be able to walk away with $100,000 in cash to put into another turnaround; I will not agree to staying with the firm for a period of more than six months after closing."

That's all there is to an exit plan. But notice that quite a bit of work and thought goes into its development.

There is one final issue you need to confront. Essentially you are an investor, an active investor, a *very active investor,* in this business you will buy. All good investors in the stock market put a "stop loss" on their investments. That means, as you know, that they sell the stock if it drops to or below a certain level. This is an important step for you to take. There is less risk in the kind of investing you will be doing because you will do a very careful financial analysis and you will be able to apply your business talents to the turnaround. But things can go sour! The economy, local or national, can turn down. An unexpected technology can arise that creates problems for part of your business. There are all the normal risks in business (discussed in Chapter 9). You need to put a stop-loss on the business based on your business plan. By monitoring the financials of the company on a monthly basis, you will be able to track the trends of sales and profits. If they begin to head south, you need to say, "Enough. It's time to sell and get out what money we can." Your team of accountant, lawyer, and financial planner are vital here because they will give you an objective opinion. I can absolutely guarantee that you will want to hang on longer than any of your advisors. You will fall in love with the business or else your ego will insist that you can make it grow and be profitable. Put those feelings aside and listen to that team of friendly experts who have your best interests at heart.

Business Planning

Everybody says you should do a business plan when you start or operate a company. It is more important when you buy one. There are three reasons to pursue this discipline:

- *To help you make the decision on whether to invest in this particular company.*

- *To guide you through the turnaround process.*

- *To serve as a sale tool when you get ready to sell.*

Take those reasons one at a time.

Your analysis of the financial statements indicated that the business had the potential to be a profitable turnaround for you. The next big question is this: how should this be done and how long will it take? Remember that the ideal turnaround candidate is one that takes the minimum amount of time. Buy a company that needs an investment in time and money to develop new markets or new products, and you buy the problem of putting more money into it and then waiting, with some risk, for the investment to pay off. So you need to do a business plan in order to assess whether or not the company merits your final offer. *Never buy a business without creating a preliminary business plan for it.*

The decision on whether or not to buy can be based on a preliminary business plan. You need to compute some financial numbers and do some conservative estimating on markets and market shares, cost of goods sold, and fixed expenses (see the paragraphs on this item later in this chapter). You need to see if there are places where expenses, variable and fixed, can be cut. A few hours should provide insight into what it will take to make the turnaround work.

To implement the turnaround you need a more detailed business plan. Here the requirement is to establish quarterly and annual projections and goals. The plan will include such matters as revised staffing, new sales and marketing programs, product quality improvement efforts, and so on. This more detailed plan produces a set of action items that must be accomplished.

But the most critical and important reason for creating a good detailed business plan is that it becomes part of your sales package when you are ready to sell the business. Remember that we discussed the problems facing the naive seller and one of them is the lack of information about what the company *will be worth* at some point in the future. That is what a business plan does. It says to the buyer: if you do this and this and this, then the sales of the company will increase to this level and the cash flow stream will produce this much total income for you over the next five years. That becomes the basis for valuing the company. Your accountant can translate the effect of the cash flow stream on the balance sheet to show the increase in book value over the same time period.

So begin with a rudimentary plan that allows you to make a decision on whether or not to buy. If you do proceed with the deal, flesh out the plan so that it becomes a guide for you to accomplish the turn-around. And as the process moves on, refine and revise the plan so that it becomes a part of the total sales package made available to potential acquirers in the future.

The Prose Section of the Business Plan

A typical business plan document consists of a prose and financial section. The prose part provides qualitative information on the business and usually consists of the following sections:

- business purpose or objectives

- history

- management

- product or service offered

- selling and marketing strategy

- plant and facilities

- labor force

- competition

- administration

Your naive seller will rarely have completed a business plan, and if one exists, it is probably out of date.

Prior to acquisition, you need to make sure you understand the history, product or service offered, selling and marketing strategy, and the competition. These become the basis for projections into the future on sales and costs. Those items, in turn, are used in the financial portion of the plan. The information on the competition provides a basis for assessing competitive risks.

After you buy the business, you need to develop the full plan including all of the sections listed above. At that time you should describe how you intend to define the mission of the organization, how you will implement a management strategy, what you will do in terms of product development, what you will do in marketing and sales strategies, improvements you intend to make in the plant and facilities, changes in the labor force, and shifts in the administrative processes.

When you are ready to sell, the plan should be updated to show the next prospective owner what needs to be done in the next several years.

The business objectives section includes statements on the expect growth rate of the business, the overall product and market development strategy, and the deployment of resources. Since you are engaged in a turnaround, this section should state explicitly how you expect to be able to increase sales and decrease costs, the time frame involved, and your expected return from those activities.

The history of the business will be an important section of the plan document when you try to sell the business. A concise story is needed here with particular emphasis on the recent past. Of course, it is useful to know that the business has been operating successfully for thirty years, if that is the case. Yet there is no need to go into great detail about the past. Always keep in mind that the astute buyer is purchasing the future of the company, not the past. The history sets the stage for your anticipation about the future.

Management of the company has consisted of the prior owner and his or her team. There is no need for you to spend a lot of time on this section if you intend to change the management procedures and style. You should described the changes and what they will accomplish. Again, you will need to make this a strong yet concise description when it comes time to sell.

The discussion of the products or services offered is critical to the acquisition, turnaround, and eventual re-sale of the business. You must understand what it is that the business does! That may seem elementary, and yet too many people buy a small business without really understanding the products or services.

Of particular interest to you and an eventual subsequent buyer are the technical issues surrounding the products or services. What makes them unique in the market place? What trade secrets does the company possess to provide a competitive advantage? Have there been or could there improvements and developments to provide a competitive advantage?

For example, one company manufactured a product that was unique and the only one of its type available for that particular application. Originally, the product had been patented. That protection ran out several years prior to the sale of the company, but the product had no competition. The reason was that the market was relatively small and it would cost a competitor too much to attempt a market entry at this late date. That kind of information needs to be part of your understanding of the business and later needs to be communicated forcefully to another buyer.

Probably the most important part of the prose portion of the business plan comes next: selling and marketing. The reason is that the financial projections are heavily dependent on the expected sales volumes for various products or services. In the paragraphs below on the financial part of the plan, increasing sales is one of the obvious ways to add value to a company. But that requires some kind of marketing and selling plan.

This part of the plan should pinpoint as clearly as possible the potential end users. Then it should describe the benefits to the customers of the products or service. These are the fundamentals of the marketing plan. From that basic information, the plan must describe the ways in which potential customers will be made aware of the product - through newspaper, magazine, or direct mail advertising, as examples. For a small business, the plan should deal with low cost or free ways to get publicity which include articles in newspapers or magazines, demonstrations at community events, and speeches or seminars. Marketing materials such as brochures, fliers, newsletters, product sheets, and so on need to be addressed in the plan which must also address the distribution channels to be used. Will the product be sold through distributors? Retail stores? Direct through mail order? Or what?

This blends in with the selling strategies. Here the plan must discuss the use of salaried or commission sales people in the company or else ways to retain a sales force outside of the company. The discounts and commissions need to be explained so that they can be factored into the financial projections.

A major part of the marketing and business plan should be an analysis of the competition. The prices, customer service, distribution channels, and other aspects of competitors' business practices should be outlined. A lack of understanding of the competition - and how to fight it - spells doom for the small business. A competent review of the competition should suggest niches which can be exploited, and niche marketing is the hallmark of the successful company.

There are a few other items which are put into most business plans. The plant, store, warehouse, facilities, and equipment should be described with particular emphasis on items that represent a competitive advantage or items which need to be replaced or updated.

A similar description of the labor force is required. The prevailing hourly rates, productivity levels, competencies, and training opportunities represent significant factors influencing the profitability of a business. This section of the plan can also deal with the labor market in the area where the business is located.

Finally, the administrative processes of the business need to be assessed. In some businesses, the ability to track business processes by means of paperwork or computer software is vital. FedEx and UPS have revolutionized shipping because of their ability to find out exactly where a shipment is located at any time of the day or night. Effective small businesses are able to find out quickly how and what they are doing, not only from accounting data, but also in terms of the flow of work through the company.

The Financial Section of the Business Plan

The detailed financial plan for a purchased company is somewhat easier to work out than for a start-up. You have the financials for the last three to five years, and that is a good starting point.

You must keep in mind that your goal is to increase the profitability and income stream of the business in order to sell it for a good gain. The structure of an income statement provides all the clues you need for your turnaround financial plan. Remember that the income statement (or P&L) consists of the following major categories:

Sales

Cost of goods sold

Fixed expenses

Interest expenses

Taxes

Those are your five strategic keys.

The first and most obvious way to improve results is *to increase sales*. You can project a reasonable increase in your forecast financial but that increase should be based on a detailed and complete marketing plan. You will need to know the total current market, your share of it, the competition, and then have a plan for how to increase your share. The other option is to look for new markets for existing products or for new products to introduce into the existing market.

The next two moves *involve cost reduction* and control. *"Cost of goods sold"* is a measure of the efficiency of the operation. Anything that will improve efficiency will cut these costs. Much of modern management in the last two decades has been directed at reducing cost of goods sold and these methods include total quality management, integrated product teams, and similar techniques. In your plan, you will need to estimate a reasonable improvement in efficiency, how you will attain it, and the effect on cost of goods sold.

In small businesses, the *fixed* expenses are often bloated. This happens over the years as the owner is sold on various programs and plans. Rarely does a new item in the fixed expense budget kick out an old item. The new one is just added on. You can look over the fixed expense items for the business and make an estimate as to how many dollars could be saves by eliminating unnecessary or redundant items. Also keep in mind that this is where many of the perks of the owner appear. You can eliminate those perks because your goal is to make the company worth more and not to take cash out as an owner and manager.

At the bottom of an income statement there is usually a space for interest and other non-operating expenses (and income). Take a careful look at this area. You - with your superior understanding of business and finance - may be able to eliminate or at least minimize interest expenses.

Finally, your accountant should assist you in seeing if there are ways in which you can take advantage of tax breaks which will improve the performance of the company. Again, keep in mind that most small business owners operate in a way to minimize the tax impact on their personal income and, at the same time, on the business. Your target is to maximize the total cash flow of the business in a way that is easy to demonstrate to a potential buyer. In developing your turnaround business plan, discuss with your accountant ways in which the taxes can be minimized and the cash flow maximized.

Any one of these five strategies will improve the financial condition of the company. All five, taken together, should produce a sizable increase in the cash flow and, eventually, in the net worth of the business. A well written business plan provides the basis for understanding the potential of each of these strategies in turning the business around.

Behind any financial projection in a business plan are a set of assumptions. The two absolutely key parts of the financial plan are the projected income statements for the next three to five years and the cash flow projection for the same time period. Income statements show the potential for a cash flow stream which then becomes a major part of the valuation of the business upon re-sale. The cash flow projection is needed in order to find out if the business can be turned around on its own or whether it will need an infusion of cash *after the acquisition by you.* Obviously, that last item is very important. If you have limited financial resources and expend most of them on the purchase, you will not be able to accomplish the turnaround because you won't have the cash to do it.

In order to generate a projected income statement for the years ahead, you need first to make an assumption about sales. Since this is an operating enterprise, you have the history of the last three to five years. Your task is to extrapolate into the future on some reasonable basis. This is done based upon the marketing and sales plan in the prose section of the business plan. Normally you will plan on some growth in sales. You - and a subsequent buyer - should be comfortable in projecting some kind of increase. It is foolish to make this projection too optimistic. You shouldn't base your turnaround and profit potential on unrealistic projections.

If you are not certain about the sales projections, then you need to retain a marketing consultant for enough time to produce a sensible estimate of market penetration, market share, and similar matters. *Don't just take a wild guess!* Unfortunately, that is the basis for many sales projections, and that is the reason many small businesses fail.

After you estimate the sales volumes for various products and services and multiply those times prices, you will obtain probable gross sales dollars for each year in the future. The next step is to make an assumption about the variable costs or costs of goods sold. You do have history here. You can and probably should assume that you can introduce some efficiencies into the operations of the company.

These may be fairly small. Variable costs may represent 70% of gross sales over the last three years, and you can assume that you can reduce those costs to 69%, 68%, and 67% over the next three years. If you calculate the effect of those reductions, you will find that they usually result in large increases in profit.

Then you should take a careful look at the fixed expenses of the business. This is where the person from whom you are buying the business may have loaded up on perks such as insurance policies, retirement plans, travel expenses, and similar items. You can and should reduce these. Furthermore, you may be able to buy insurance at lower prices than the owner. You may be able to achieve economies by shopping around for office supplies, long distance telephone services, advertising services, and on and on. Again, assume a modest decrease in these costs and calculate the effect on the bottom line.

To review, I suggest that you make your best educated estimate on sales, variable costs, and fixed costs - the "big three" determinants of the profit before interest and taxes. These represent the basis for your turnaround plan, and the results of your computations should show you that the plan is feasible - or that it is not. Don't buy the company if reasonable assumptions produce results that will not create wealth for you. Move on to another candidate business.

The second critical item in the quantitative part of your plan is the cash flow projection. An income statement is a snapshot of the income over a period of time - a month, quarter, or year. You can show a pretty healthy profit for a year and still have financial problems because of cash flow. The reason, of course, is that most businesses use the accrual accounting method. That means that a sale is booked when the invoice is sent out to the customer, not when the money is received. There is a lag between those two events. In some businesses, such as construction, there can be a large time lag between completion of work which results in an invoice and the date on which the check is put in the bank.

While that lag in income is occurring, you have to continue to pay bills. The payroll comes due. Your suppliers want to be paid. Certainly the IRS and state revenue department want their tax checks on time. The difference between the flow of money in and the flow out means that you have to have some money available. That is known as the operating capital of the business. For some kinds of businesses, the operating capital can be fairly low. For others, it is quite high. The latter occurs when the payments come in slowly while the bills have to be paid quickly.

As part of your business plan, you need to create a cash flow projection, month by month, for the first year and on a yearly basis after that. This will give you some idea as to the cash that will be needed to operate the business. You will have to provide that cash. Don't spend all your cash on the purchase and then find out that you can't run the business! It does you no good to have to file bankruptcy for the company six months after you buy it.

The cash flow projection depends on two assumptions: cash collections and cash disbursements. Again you have a history because you are looking at an operating enterprise. You are one up on the individual trying to start a business. Using the historical data, you should be able to come up with reasonable estimates about collections and disbursements. One thing to keep in mind, though: if you intend to grow the business, you will need more operating capital than if it just remained static.

So figure in the growth in sales. This will have a big effect on cash flow. You will have to buy the merchandise for re-sale or you will have to purchase raw materials and components in order to manufacture products. That money will flow out before the merchandise or products results in collections. Growth can be expensive! Be sure to do those calculations and use conservative estimates - long delays in getting paid, short times to make payments.

Based on the income statement and the current balance sheet of the business, your accountant can create projected balance sheets for the three to five years ahead. These will be helpful because they will show how good the business will look to someone who focuses on net worth rather than income stream.

There is one final financial item to consider in your turnaround plan. Some businesses require a capital investment in order to become more profitable. That usually comes about because equipment and facilities need to be updated. If this is true for the business you are thinking about buying, factor it into the overall business plan.

The Plan of Reorganization in a Bankruptcy

This document has been discussed previously in the section on buying businesses in Chapter 11 bankruptcy, but some of the information bears repeating here. One fact should be clear to you: a plan of reorganization is *not a business plan*. Keep that in mind.

The plan of reorganization is a document intended for use by the creditors of the bankrupt business and the bankruptcy court so that they can satisfy themselves that there will be money to pay off the creditors.

Remember that the plan of reorganization first classifies the creditors as secured, priority, and unsecured. Then the plan should show how each class of creditor will be paid. Some may be paid in full within a short period of time, usually the secured creditors. However, even the secured creditors may be asked to negotiate to be paid less than the full debt. Then the priority creditors need to paid off in some way and over a specified period of time. Finally, the unsecured creditors will almost certainly be paid cents on the dollar over a long period of time - if they are paid at all. Hopefully they will agree to a long payout period of a small amount of money because the ongoing business will provide them with payments for goods and services in the future. They can make money from an operating business as a customer, and the alternative is usually a liquidation in which they get little or nothing in the near term and are certain of getting nothing at all in the future.

The final part of the plan of reorganization is a discussion of how the money to pay off the creditors will be obtained or generated. At this point, the plan of reorganization and the business plan overlap, quite obviously. You had better know and put into your business plan where and how you are going to get the money to pay creditors and create the turnaround.

Again, the point is that a good business plan automatically creates the basis for a plan of reorganization. You should also be aware that a plan of reorganization based upon a solid business plan is certain to be received favorably by the creditors and court, more favorably than one that seems to just be thrown together.

The Return on Your Investment

In addition to the traditional business plan, as I have just described, you and your financial advisor have one additional task to complete: to estimate your probable return from the purchase, turnaround, and sale of the business. Using the three estimates of discounted cash flow - high, low, and most probably - run a quick calculation to find out what your selling price will be for all three conditions. In other words, work up a best, worst, and middle estimate of what you will get out of the business when you sell. Then compute the return on investment. The big question is whether this return is worth the risk involved in the process.

Savvy investors know that the stock market, over the long term, returns roughly 11% - pre-tax. On the low side you can get 4-6% virtually risk-free from U.S. Government treasuries or insured bank investments. Venture capitalists look for returns on the order of 20-30%. Realistically, you should expect to get at least a 15% return on your investment and possibly more. If you get less than 15%, you could get the same return with less risk by sticking the money in a good mutual fund for a reasonable period of time. So if your initial investment is, say, $50,000, and it takes three years to turn the business around and sell it, you should expect, at 15%, to clear around $76,000 for a profit of

$26,000. At 20%, you would get $85,000 and a profit of $35,000. And you would see a gain of $47,000 at 25%. (Keep in mind while looking at these numbers that you would be paid a salary as the manager of the business; these returns are on the initial investment and don't include salary.)

The return on the investment also depends, quite clearly, on the total investment you are required to make. That will consist of three items: the cash needed to purchase the business, any additional cash needed for operating capital, and, finally, the cash required for capital investments to produce growth. For example, one recent deal involved a cash payment of $45,000 to the owner, but the financial projections indicated that the new owner would have to put in an additional $20,000 in operating capital to handle the anticipated growth in the company plus an investment of $7,500 for an up-to-date piece of equipment. The total investment was $72,500.

The "big picture" here is that you need to develop an initial business plan before you make the decision to buy and then need to add details after purchase as you work out the complete turnaround plan. The business plan should continue to be updated so that it provides a basis for you to develop a selling price for the company that maximizes your return. Along with the business plan you need to create an exit plan, one that sets goals for how long you intend to work the turnaround, your relationship to the company after its re-sale, and the amount and kind of monetary return you expect.

■

Chapter 11

MAKING AN OFFER AND STRUCTURING THE DEAL

Here is where your advisory team is important. Structuring a business purchase can be a very complex matter. In this chapter we'll go over some of the options. You need to understand them in order to discuss these matters intelligently with your lawyer, accountant, and financial planner.

The current form of business for the company you want to buy - proprietorship, partnership, or corporation - will dictate some of the features of an acquisition deal. A proprietorship is the easiest for obvious reasons. You are dealing with a single individual who owns the business and he or she can make all the decisions. A partnership, on the other hand, requires the approval of both or all of the partners. You may find yourself embroiled in a dispute among the partners which could delay and complicate the whole situation. The most complex situation is when you deal with an incorporated entity, and the next section discusses the two major forms of acquisition: asset and stock purchase.

Asset versus Stock Purchase

There are two basic ways to buy a business that is incorporated: an asset purchase or a stock purchase. Pros and cons exist for each method. Most common is the asset purchase. You will probably end up with an asset purchase, and that form is most beneficial to you as a buyer.

In an asset purchase, you literally buy the assets of the target company, not the stock. That means you buy the receivables, inventory, prepaid expenses, equipment, facilities, and real estate. Whatever is listed on the balance sheet as an asset. Don't get too excited, here, because you also "buy" the liabilities on the balance sheet. In other words, you take on the commitment to pay the payables, notes, leases, and other monies owed to outsiders. As I discussed in detail in the section on valuation, you hope to buy the assets at a price below fair market value.

There is an additional advantage to you in buying the assets of a business even for a value higher than that shown on the balance sheet. The accounting basis for those assets is cost, what the business paid for the asset when it was purchased. That basis is then adjusted for depreciation. However, when you buy an asset, there is a new "basis:" what you paid for it. You can now depreciate the asset from the new basis. This will add to your bottom line results.

The advantages of an asset sale are that it is a fairly straightforward way to handle an acquisition and can be done with cash and notes. No stock issuances or transfers are needed. The major disadvantage is that completing the deal is complex because each and every asset must be conveyed separately. That means a lot of paper work and lots of involvement by lawyers and accountants. In addition, all of the shareholders have to approve the sale of the business. There will also be state and local transfer taxes to be paid.

There is a legal advantage to the asset purchase. Product and service liability for all business transactions prior to the sale remain with the seller. You will "buy" the financial obligations and liabilities but not be responsible for actions taken by the management or ownership before the sale.

Just the opposite occurs if you do a stock purchase. In this case, you make an offer to the shareholders at so many dollars per share. If that is acceptable, they turn the stock certificates over to you, and you write them checks. You do, in this case, take on all of the liabilities of the corporation. The major advantage of a stock purchase is that it is simple and can be done quickly. There is minimal need for extended legal or accounting services.

Most small business acquisitions, where a corporate entity is involved, are done with an asset purchase rather than a stock purchase. The main reasons are the potential tax advantages accruing from the adjusted basis of the assets and the fact that legal liabilities are not transferred in the sale.

Mergers

Of course, there is always the possibility of a merger. This had some real advantages to the sellers because, properly handled, a merger is not a taxable event. In other words, the seller does not have to pay taxes, ordinary income or capital gains, if her or his company is merged into another one.

To accomplish a merger, you have to create an entity of your own into which you can merge the target company. This usually means incorporating with the capital you have received from family, friends, and other investors. A problem here is that you don't have an ordinary operating business. You have actually created an investment company unless you can figure out some small operation to undertake. This could involve simply setting up a minimal mail order business or something similar. Your attorney and accountant will have to advise you on these matters because setting up an investment company is quite different from establishing an operating business. Actually there were a number of companies set up during the 1980's called "blind pools." They were pools of money obtained from investors. Blind because at the time the money was invested no one knew what kind of operating business would be purchased or established. Blind pools consisting of public money are difficult to set up - thank goodness - in the current business environment. You can check with your advisory team to see if it is feasible to create one using private placement money.

However, a merger probably is not all that beneficial to you as a purchaser unless you already own a well-financed and profitable small business of your own. Growing that business through merger is a different topic than making money by buying and selling small businesses, the topic of this book.

Summary of Pros and Cons of Asset or Stock Sale or a Merger

The *advantages of a* <u>stock sale</u> for both the buyer and seller are: simple to execute, can be done quickly, management objections are not a factor if managers hold shares, and no vote of shareholders is required.

There are *disadvantages to the buyer:* liabilities, including those which are unknown or contingent, transfer to the buyer; may have to deal with minority shareholders if the acquired corporation is to be liquidated after purchase, and there is a lot of work to be done.

The *disadvantages to the seller* can include: majority stockholder may have a fiduciary duty to minority shareholders; could require an SEC registration; and may involve stock ownership in the acquiring company.

The major advantage to the seller is: liabilities transfer to the buyer.

For an <u>asset sale</u>, the *advantage* for both the buyer and seller is that this is a straightforward sale.

There are disadvantages to the asset sale: complexity of the legal documents; can take a long time, requires favorable votes of most of the shareholders; may be transfer taxes involved; must comply with bulk sales law.

The *advantages to the buyer* are: liabilities do not transfer with the sale and only the desired assets are purchased. *There are disadvantages to the buyer* in addition to those for both the buyer and seller: cannot use stock in addition to cash and notes for purchase, must not violate creditors' rights, possible disruption of customers and suppliers.

The *disadvantages to the seller* are those listed for both buyer and seller.

Although not common in deals with small businesses, _mergers_ do have a place. They have the following advantages for both buyer and seller: straightforward deal legally and assets are transferred by operation of law

The *disadvantages* for both are: dissenting minority shareholders have appraisal rights, shareholders of both companies must approve, and the acquired company may lose its identity.

Negatives for the buyer include: hidden or contingent liabilities are assumed and warranties and representations made by the seller do not survive the transaction.

For the *seller,* there are *two advantages:* a wide range of considerations (cash, stock, notes) can be received and an opportunity may exist to participate in the growth of the combined entity.

The latter is also a potential disadvantage. If part or all of the consideration is in the form of shares in the acquiring company, there is also an opportunity to participate in a reduction in value!

These listings of pros and cons are important for

you as a buyer to understand from your own perspective but also vital in terms of understanding the seller's benefits and risks.

After all of this, I need to say that a large majority of small business transactions are asset sales. Yet you should be aware of your options in structuring and proposing a deal.

Cash Payments, Owner Carryback, and Stock

Deal structures for small businesses range from "all cash" to a small amount of cash and a large owner carryback note to the seller. What are the pros and cons?

Well the first and most obvious is how much money you have available versus how much the acquisition will cost. If your assessment shows that the business is worth $200,000 and you only have $75,000, then you will have to get the owner - or someone - to lend you the difference, $125,000, for some period of time. And you may want to use only $50,000 of your cash and hold the remainder for other business purposes. That $25,000 may be needed for an improved marketing effort or a product improvement program.

In most cases, you are better off putting less down and getting the owner to lend you the maximum he or she is willing to offer. The reason is simply the leverage that this provides. I pointed this out in Chapter 1. If you can buy a business with $25,000 in cash and sell it three years later for a gain of $50,000, you have doubled your money in that time period. If you had to spend $100,000 to buy the same business and it still took three years to turn it around and sell it for a gain of $50,000, you have a much smaller relative gain.

Is there a situation where an all-cash deal might appeal? Yes. If you chance on one of the extremely under-valued businesses discussed in Chapter 13 on the fastest turnarounds, you are better off buying it outright. This is true because you are going to perform some magic on the financial statements and put it right back on the market. You don't want the previous owner looking over your shoulder and suddenly realizing what he or she had be missed out on! Better to get the business free and clear and then proceed with your turnaround plan.

Key negotiating points in an owner carryback loan will be the length of the note, the interest rate, and any balloon payments. A smart seller will want a fairly high interest rate because there is some risk involved in the loan. In fact, the risk is about the same as the risk you are undertaking in buying and running the business. Remember that the overall stock market return is something like 11% over a long period of time. That is normally well above the prime interest rate charged by banks. However, the typical seller will usually settle for some formula like "prime plus 2%." How big the "plus" is depends on the financial smarts of the seller. You should offer "prime" or "prime plus 2." Negotiate from there.

The length of the note and balloon payments are of interest to both parties, you and the seller. Again, a smart seller will realize that money paid several years from now is not worth as much as money paid up front. This is the issue of discounted cash flow. The longer the term of the note, the greater the total discount. From your standpoint, the note should be as long as possible. From the seller's viewpoint, it should be as short as possible or it should include a balloon payment after three to five years.

You want the longest time possible because that reduces the principal and interest that have to be paid each year, items which are a cash drain on the company. It might be possible to negotiate an "interest only" note for the first three years, but that usually will require larger payments on principal later or a single large balloon payment somewhere downstream. Some buyers are even able to negotiate a loan from the seller in which no interest or principal payments are made for the first several years.

This is an area where you and your advisory team need to talk things out very thoroughly. If you think you can turn the business around fairly fast and need cash flow to do it, then an "interest only" or "no interest or principal" note for the first three years might make sense. On the other hand, the seller may need that cash flow for personal purposes.

There are other ways in which the seller can be compensated as part of the deal. If the seller's knowledge, expertise, or contacts are important to the business and needed during the transition to your ownership and management, you can hire the seller as an employee for six months or so. The problem with that is the business will have to pay the various payroll taxes. Therefore, it is more common to have the seller retained as a consultant to the business for some period of time.

It is also commonplace to pay the seller an annual amount to sign a non-compete agreement. This is a legal arrangement and provides the seller with a cash income for the period of the agreement.

The structure of a deal can include the cash payment, a carryback note from the seller, an employment or consulting agreement, and payments for signing a non-compete agreement. Added together, all of these payments represent the price of the business to the seller. However, the ongoing payments must come out of the cash flow of the company, and you need to figure that into your calculations and turnaround plan.

Finally do not overlook the possibility of using stock in your company as part of the payment. This comes under the heading of a merger. If you have a corporation or partnership, you can offer the seller participation in the new combined entity. This might work if the seller sees some possibility of gain from such an arrangement.

Sources of Money Other Than the Owner

In the preceding section I pointed out that most deals involve some combination of cash and notes, the latter usually carried by the previous owner. There is also the possibility, somewhat remote, of using stock in your corporation as part of the deal.Other sources of money exist. If the business you are going to buy does not have a lot of debt, you can borrow money from a bank or other lending agency. A little knowledge of finances and the ability to analyze financial statements helps here. Lenders will look at the ratio of debt to total assets and debt to equity, that is, the dollar value of loans versus the dollar value of assets (as carried on the books) or stock in a business. If there isn't much in the way of debt compared to equity, say ten percent or less, there may be a possibility of asking for a loan.

The lender will also look at a factor known as "times interest earned." This is the ratio of earnings, before interest and taxes, to the interest expense on the income statement. The question here is: to what extent is the business able to service its debt? If the earnings are ten or twenty times the interest expense, then there is room for more debt.

Security is the major concern of the lender. No one will lend - at least at any reasonable interest rate - without some kind of collateral. The lender wants some assurance that part of the money lent can be recouped in the event of a default.

If the business you are going to buy has relatively little debt, you may be able to arrange a line of credit or short term note by pledging receivables and inventory as collateral. Banks differ in how much they will lend on receivables and inventory. You can bet that it isn't 100%! If the business you want to acquire has fairly low debt, you may be able to get a lender to give you anywhere from 40% to 60% of the receivables and inventory. The exact percentage will depend on the lender's assessment of the receivables and inventory. For example, receivables on government contracts are fairly certain to be paid. It just takes a long time. On the other hand, receivables from a cluster of small businesses in an economically depressed area will not look too promising. Current economic conditions, locally and nationally, will influence the lender's decision.

Inventory value will also depend on economic conditions, the state of the industry in which the business is operating, and the age and value of the actual articles in the inventory.

There is also a trick used by some of the "big guys" in the business world that you can consider: an asset sale and lease back. If the business you are looking at has some fairly large fixed assets on its books, there may be a way to sell those assets to someone and then lease them back. This generates cash which can be used to operate the business, develop new products, or open up new markets.

Tax Considerations

This is where life gets complicated and you need the advice of your attorney, accountant, and financial planner. However you should be aware of the potential positive effect of an asset purchase. In that case, you can establish a new basis for the assets you bought.

Here's the way it works. Suppose you agree to pay $100,000 for the business in a combination of cash and notes. After the deal, you and your accountant get to value the assets at a new cost basis. That will usually be higher than they were carried on the books of the business. You will then be able to depreciate those assets using whatever favorable depreciation schedule the IRS will allow. This will, in effect, provide you with an additional source of cash flow in the years ahead. Depreciation results in cash flow in this way. The income statement shows some dollar value for the depreciation of assets each year. The dollar amount is subtracted from the gross income. However, you as a business owner do not write a check to anyone for that amount. It is strictly an accounting move and no cash changes hands. The income statement will show an "expense" of say $5,000 in depreciation which will reduce the net profit by that amount. But the $5,000 isn't paid to anyone and doesn't go anywhere.

In his excellent book *Mergers & Acquisitions,* Joseph Marren shows how to calculate the Net Present Tax Cost (NPTC) of a purchase. The model suggests that if you structure a deal properly, the NPTC is less than the purchase price. Conversely, it is important to understand the Net Present Proceeds (NPP) for the seller, a topic which I discuss a little later in this chapter.

Another tax consideration you need to understand is that of goodwill. In general terms, goodwill is the money paid for a business above and beyond what it is worth on the balance sheet. This should not be a problem for you in most cases because you will try to buy the business at the balance sheet net worth or even at a discount to that value. There may be a case, however, where you will pay a premium. Say the cash flow analysis indicates the business is worth more than the balance sheet indicates. If you pay more than the balance sheet value, there will be some goodwill. That is not good for you as the buyer because goodwill must be amortized over a long period of time.

In structuring the deal, you can avoid goodwill by offering the owner a consulting agreement, a non-compete agreement, or continued employment as part of the package. If the business is worth $250,000 on the books, you offer $200,000 in cash and note plus a $90,000 non-compete agreement for a period of three years. The seller gets an apparent $290,000 or $40,000 more than the book value, but for tax purposes you only paid $200,000.

The other standard way to avoid goodwill is to include intangible assets or intellectual property rights in the deal. Again, your lawyer and accountant should help you in this regard.

Here is another consideration for you to use in making your offer to the seller. The business may have had one or more years with a net operating loss, an N.O.L. to lawyers and accountants. If the owner kept the business, that N.O.L. could be "carried forward" for tax purposes and the business would not have to pay corporate income taxes or at least pay minimal taxes for some years in the future. Unfortunately, you cannot "buy" the N.O.L. It doesn't transfer to you with the sale of the business. But it may have an advantage to the seller. The sale of the business will be a taxable event, and the seller will have to pay capital gains taxes if the selling price is higher than her or his investment in the company. It may be that the N.O.L. can be used to offset some of the tax liability resulting from the sale. This is something you and your accountant and lawyer should analyze and then point out to the seller as part of your negotiating strategy.

Looking At It From the Seller's Viewpoint

Every good negotiator steps into the shoes of the person on the other side of the table. What are the self-interests of the person with whom you are dealing? You should have a pretty good idea of this from your interviews and conversations with the seller.

If that individual wants to get out of the business in the worst way, whether due to ultimate boredom or financial problems. There will be little motivation to stay around and help you if boredom is the problem and there will be a lot of motivation to get as much cash up front as possible if there are personal financial difficulties. Trying to counter these motivational issues will be difficult. The seller who wants a lot of cash is not going to listen to your scheme for a note with no interest or principal payments and a balloon in five years. You will need to maximize the cash up front or walk away from the deal.

Cost and Investment Analysis

After you have completed an initial draft of the deal as you would like to have it structured, the time has come to get back to investment basics. You need to look at the cost of the purchase: what is the total dollar amount that is involved? Is it reasonable in terms of the value of the business that you calculated earlier? That is the first question.

The second part of the equation is to look at the amount of money you actually invest. With any kind of owner carryback, some portion of the total cost will be paid out of the cash flow of the business. The amount of money, usually cash, that you put up to buy the business is your investment. Your goal is to make money with that money.

Risk and Return Analysis

The other side of any investment - and remember that you are getting into this as an investment, not as a career or a lifetime way to make a salary - is the return you are likely to get and what risks are involved in getting it.

A good way to do this analysis is to return to your business plan and estimate the best, worst, and most probable payoffs. The best payoff is a quick turn-around with a fairly large increase in the value of the business, say a value 150% higher in three years. The worst payoff involves a much longer time period, maybe five to seven years, and a 50% increase in value. Somewhere in between is a most probable pay-off, in the example I am using here, a 100% increase in value in four years. Using a simple financial calcula-tor to get the results, the three scenarios provide the following returns: best, 35%; most probable, 19%; worst, 6%.

The other part of this analysis is to evaluate the risks involved compared to the returns. To get a return of 19% in the stock market - over a four year period - would be pretty phenomenal. It could happen if you were lucky enough to hit a bull market for most of that period, but you would be more likely to see a total return of closer to 10%. You might be a little higher or lower than that. The 35% would be great but you have to be realistic with yourself and understand that the odds are low you will be able to get that return. On the low side, the 6% return is what you could get by investing in very safe treasuries. So this deal appears to be somewhat favorable and worthy of you proceeding.

If the numbers came out showing a best estimate of 20%, a most probable of 10%, and a worst case of a small loss, you would be well advised to put that money into the stock market - or on another business - because the returns are not worth the risk.

There is no easy way to quantify the risks. In Chapter 9, I covered some of the more common risks in running a business together with actions that can be taken to minimize them. So you need to go back and look over those risk factors and your ability to control them.

At this point, you must be hard-nosed investor. It will be very easy to "fall in love" with the potential of the business. You can see yourself sitting behind the desk in the front office with everything running smoothly and the money piling up in the cash drawer. This is fantasy time. Step back and look carefully at the cost, investment, risk, and return numbers. Would an astute investor go for this deal or not? If you aren't sure, then check it out with a couple of people who might be potential investors. Get their opinions and impressions. If they would invest, that is a good sign you should do the same. If they seem hesitant and start raising objections, listen very carefully.

I must keep reminding you that your intent is to make money from buying and selling small businesses. Keep that goal in mind at all times. Stay focused on it. Believe the numbers. Believe the opinions of your advisory team.

Making the Offer

The offer should be presented in writing to the business owner and should outline the terms and conditions. There is no need to go into great detail. For example, an offer letter might be worded like this:

Dear...

The purpose of this letter is to make an offer for an asset purchase of your business, the XYZ Corp. I will be able to provide you with $50,000 in cash upon closing. I would need to have you remain in a consulting capacity with the firm for a period of six months at a retainer of $20,000 for that time. In addition, you will receive an annual payment of $25,000 for a period of three years as compensation for a non-compete agreement. In order to complete the purchase, I would need to have you carry a note for $89,500 for a period of five years at an interest rate equal to prime plus 2% at the time of closing. Payments on the note would be made quarterly and include interest and principal payments. The total offer is, therefore, worth $234,500 plus the interest payments on the note which we estimate to total an additional $54,500.

This offer is nonbinding and contingent upon performance of due diligence.

Very truly yours,

Of course your lawyer will want to draft the letter for your particular circumstances, and your accountant and financial planner will be a part of structuring the deal.

Negotiating Strategy

Remember the overall process here. You started out by making an offer via letter that was non-binding. Then you performed due diligence and created a business plan in addition to your personal exit plan. I discussed, briefly, the pros and cons in making a final offer. It may be higher, the same as, or lower than your initial offer in dollar terms, and you may want to exclude certain assets or liabilities after due diligence.

I have to keep reiterating that the owner is probably expecting to get at least the book value, if not more. You are now a sophisticated buyer, and you know that the book value, adjusted from your due diligence and analysis, is only a good number if the business is asset-rich. Normally you are buying future cash flow to make your gain and not assets to be re-sold.

The final offer usually will consist of cash, a carryback note, and perhaps some kind of non-compete or consulting agreement. You need to make sure that the total dollar value is what the owner expects, that is, the book value plus perhaps a small premium. This is the total dollar "face" value which consists of the cash, the principal and interest on the note, plus the total value of the non-compete or consulting agreement. The real value to the seller should be discounted using the discounted cash flow method, but you leave that to the seller and her or his accountant.

Here is an important consideration in entering negotiations. You have a choice of doing this face-to-face with the seller or working through your attorney or a broker. There are pros and cons both ways. If you engage in negotiations, you should be sure that you and the seller are on good terms and can negotiate without getting into serious differences. Remember that you are going to have to continue to deal with the present owner if there is a carryback note, consulting agreement, or non-compete agreement and particularly if you want to use that person as a consultant during a transition period. You certainly don't want a frustrated and angry prior owner hanging around!

The safest way to proceed is to use your attorney to do the negotiating, preferably with the seller's attorney. This distances both you and the seller from direct confrontation. You can always blame the lawyers for problems! Incidentally, this is exactly the process used by professional real estate agents. They always negotiate agent-to-agent and keep the buyers and sellers away from each other.

Whichever way you go, my advice is to "sell" your offer to the owner either personally or through your lawyer. Point out the benefits of your offer to the seller. The seller needs to know how you arrived at your offer, particularly if it differs greatly from the initial offer. Someone needs to explain, preferably in person, how assets were valued and how liabilities were figured in. Obviously you don't need to discuss your cash flow calculations or other bases for performing the valuation.

In entering negotiations, both you and your attorney need to understand some basics about that process. Traditional negotiating involved an initial offer and a range of adjustments to that offer including a point below which you would not go. This is called "positional bargaining" because each party takes a position and negotiates from that. For example, the starting point might be $225,000 total and you are willing to raise the ante to $245,000 but no higher. The seller would start at $250,000 and be willing to come down to $235,000. As long as there was this kind of overlap, a deal could be struck.

The better way to negotiate is to avoid positional bargaining. Instead, both parties establish their self-interests. You, as the buyer, have the self-interest of buying the business in a manner that permits you to turn it around and re-sell as a profit. In addition, you have some self-interests in terms of your personal life and exit plan. The seller has financial planning self-interests as well which may include retirement or some time off or enough money to start another business. Now both sides can bargain in an effort to satisfy their self-interests. This opens up the possibilities for structuring the deal in a creative manner.

There are two key concepts here: the net present tax cost of the business to you and the net present tax proceeds to the seller. These are the "real" numbers which should form the basis for negotiating. The net present cost to you is the price you pay minus any savings that result from a new cost basis for assets and the higher depreciation that you can take.

The net present tax proceeds to the seller consists of the various forms of payment minus the taxes that will be due. The seller may be liable for capital gains taxes on part of the sale and then on ordinary income taxes on other parts. However, if there had been a net operating loss (N.O.L.), he or she can use that to offset some of the taxable income. In addition, the seller should perform a discounted cash flow analysis on the income from the carryback loan principal and interest and on income from a consulting or non-compete agreement.

The seller's accountant, lawyer, and financial planner will do everything they can to minimize the tax impact and maximize the actual proceeds. They will want - or at least should want - the shortest payout period on a note and consulting or non-compete agreement. If the time periods are fairly long, they can reasonably expect to see some increase in the face value of the agreements and notes.

There may be non-financial issues, however, which encourage the seller to opt for longer term notes and agreements. If someone is thinking of retiring, it could be desirable to spread out the payments over a longer period of time. This reduces the taxable income each year and spreads the payments into lower-earning post-retirement years. In one recent example, the non-compete and consulting agreements were for a period of ten years well into the retirement years of the seller.

You, as the buyer, will want to minimize goodwill and probably pay as much as possible for fixed long term assets which we permit you to increase the depreciation write offs each year. And you will want to spread out payments on notes and agreements over the longest period of time.

Ideally, you, your advisory team, the seller and his or her advisory team would sit down together and develop the best overall deal structure for both parties. That is probably Camelot and not reality. The next best thing is to provide the best offer - for you and the seller - that you can generate and then be willing to negotiate. The more creative you and the seller can be within legal and tax limitations, the more likely you are to come up with a good deal.

■

Chapter 12

WORKING THE TURNAROUND

I once worked at a university that trained public school teachers among other professions. All of the young teachers-to-be went through at least three years of classes, training, and indoctrination. At the end of the three years, they were supposed to be prepared to go into a classroom and start teaching. One of their standard questions, just before embarking on a journey into the real world, was "But what do I do on Monday morning?" All of the theory goes out the window, and that very practical question emerges. Now you are in the same boat. You have analyzed the business, made an offer and had it accepted, you structured the deal to your satisfaction. Now you own a business. What do you do on Monday?

Setting Priorities Based on Financial Factors

This is a matter, of course, of setting priorities. One of the first things you should do is get some basic numbers planted in your head. These come from the income statement. Here is a barebones income statement:

Gross sales	=	$200,000
Cost of goods sold	=	150,000
Gross profit	=	50,000
Fixed expenses	=	30,000
Profit before		
interest and taxes	=	20,000
Interest and tax expenses	=	8,000
Net profit	=	12,000

You can increase the gross profit by increasing the gross sales or reducing the cost of goods sold, otherwise known as variable costs. The increase in gross profit will flow down to the profit before interest and taxes. You will experience an increase in the amount of taxes paid but a goodly portion of the increase in gross sales or decrease in cost of goods sold will go right down to the net profit "bottom line."

Let's take an actual example. Suppose you cut the cost of goods sold by $5,000. That moves down through the calculations and produces an increase of $5,000 in the profit before interest and taxes. As I mentioned above, you will see some increase in income taxes. Let's suppose that the taxes go up by $1,000. Now the income statement looks like this:

Gross sales	=	$200,000
Cost of good sold	=	145,000
Gross profit	=	55,000
Fixed expenses	=	30,000
Profit before		
interest and taxes	=	25,000
Interest and tax expenses	=	9,000
Net profit	=	16,000

The cost of goods sold decreased by 3.33% which resulted in an increase in net profit of $4,000 or 33.3%.

Now I have a question to ask myself as the new owner. How much would I have to increase sales in order to see the same kind of increase in net profit? In this case, I used a spreadsheet on my computer and found out that I would need to raise sales to $226,600 in order to show the same increase in profitability. That is a 13.33% increase in gross sales. Now the question is whether it is easier to increase sales 13.33% or decrease costs of goods sold by 3.33%. While the latter number is smaller, obtaining greater efficiencies may not be all that easy. If the company has been suffering from "steak with no sizzle," it may be easier to increase the gross sales number by 13.33%, at least initially.

You can increase the profit before interest and taxes by reducing the fixed expenses. A reduction of

$5,000 will produce an increase of $4,000 in net profit like this:

Gross sales	=	$200,000
Cost of good sold	=	150,000
Gross profit	=	50,000
Fixed expenses	=	25,000
Profit before		
interest and taxes	=	25,000
Interest and tax expenses	=	9,000
Net profit	=	$16,000

This is a 16.66% decrease in fixed expenses. Again, a decision has to be made on whether this is feasible or not.

Let's go through one more exercise. What if we increase sales by 2%, decrease cost of goods sold by 2%, and decrease fixed expense costs by 2%? What happens to the bottom line? That gives us an income statement like this:

Gross sales	=	$204,000
Cost of good sold	=	149,940
Gross profit	=	54,060
Fixed expenses	=	29,400
Profit before interest and taxes	=	24,660
Interest and tax expenses	=	9,864
Net profit		= $14,796

These small changes in sales and variable and fixed expenses produce an increase in profitability of 23%.

The point of all this is that a few simple calculations on the income statement numbers begins to give you a clue as to what is needed to produce an increase in profitability. The choices are some combination of an increase in sales, decrease in cost of goods sold, and decrease in fixed expenses. Depending on the particular business, the numbers will point to a particular strategy for increasing profitability.

Generally, it is best to think about trying to do all three of the strategic options: increase sales, decrease operating expenses by increasing efficiency, and decrease fixed expenses through careful budgeting and review of those expenses. But one of the areas may need more emphasis than another. One of the areas may also be easier for you - with your particularly business skills - to accomplish.

Expertise in sales and marketing will serve you well in increasing gross sales. That is pretty obvious. Managerial skills will be needed to decrease the cost of goods sold or operating expenses. You can do this by negotiating better prices from vendors, providing employees with improved equipment or machinery, and increasing the teamwork and cost consciousness of the employees. Your aim, with the employees, is to reduce scrap or waste or returns or whatever the measure is in this specific kind of business.

A reduction in fixed expenses will result, first, from careful review of those items. Can insurance premiums be reduced? Is the business over-insured? How much risk are you willing to take on in this regard? Are there ways that the utility bills can be reduced? How about office supplies? Would it be cheaper to lease or own some of the office equipment? All of these kind of questions need to be raised in looking over the fixed expenses.

Another item to consider in this modern era is whether it would be cheaper to have some services provided by contractors or contract workers. One example is bookkeeping and accounting. Does it cost less to retain someone to do that work than to keep someone on the payroll? Can some of the work in the offices be done by part-time or temporary help? It pays to be tight-fisted when it comes to the fixed expenses in a business.

Good Things to Do After Acquiring a Business

I wish I could have come up with a more elegant way to say this. I think the heading to this section is a good one, though. There are some things that you need to do after you have closed the deal and started to run the business. They are based on good business commonsense.

So part of the answer to "what do I do on Monday" is to establish your priorities in terms of increasing sales and decreasing costs. You do this based on an analysis of what is likely to pay off the fastest and easiest and an assessment of your own business skills.

Here is a list of turnaround actions that are required, sooner or later, in most small businesses. I have listed them in order of priority:

1. contact your customers and get feedback from them,

2. build an employee team,

3. build a supplier team,

4. analyze your competitive advantage,

5. revise or set up a cost accounting system,

6. review business lines for profitability,

7. establish good relations with your banker, investors, chamber of commerce, community leaders, and other stakeholders.

Remember that all of these are in addition to taking action to increase sales and reduce variable and fixed costs.

For most businesses, the first and most critical step is to contact customers to find out what they need and want. This should be done by phone or in person and not with a written survey. You want to establish a relationship with at least the key customers, and this is your golden opportunity to do just that. By direct contact, they will be able to find out who you are and what kind of person and business owner you are going to be. You will be able to listen carefully to them and follow-up on any problems or complaints they might mention. If possible set up an appointment and go visit the key customers. If that isn't possible, at least call and set up a time during which you can call back and have a lengthier discussion. You may want to visit ten key customers and then call an additional ten or twenty.

A second important action is to build an effective employee team. In due diligence, you should have gotten some insight into the employees. The first thing you need to do is identify the real contributors, the people who are okay but not highly productive, and finally those folks who are being dragged along. Here is the key to this part of the turnaround plan: you need to get rid of anyone who is not pulling her or his own weight. An effective team consists of persons who are competent and get along together. The team members are well aware of the real workers and the laggards. As the team leader, you need to weed out the laggards. That will pay off in two ways. It will eliminate their lack of productivity and at the same time serve to motivate the rest of the team who will see that you will support the people who are doing the real work.

Building a team involves leadership, and there are literally dozens of books, audiotapes, seminars, and workshops on that subject. You need to get some of that information and act on it in your new capacity at owner/manager.

There is another team you need to create: this one consists of your suppliers. Big businesses have learned this lesson very well in the past few years. Most businesses have too many suppliers, and those people don't understand your business. So the first part of this step is to review the price, delivery, and quality of the products or services each supplier provides. The goal is to whittle the number of suppliers to the smallest number who will provide a reasonable price, good delivery, and high quality. Always keep in mind the low-priced goods or service with low quality actually end up costing you more because of the hassles they create.

The second part of this step is fairly obvious but often overlooked. Supplier or subcontractors should understand your business and your customers. Too often companies just order supplies and services, and to the vendor you are just another customer "out there." Contact the key suppliers. Go to their offices. Explain to them what you do and how important their efforts are to your business success. Point out the obvious: if they help you grow, their business will grow as well. In this way, they become part of your team, and you aren't just one more account.

Plan on communicating frankly with your customers and building both an employee team and a supplier team. The next step is to identify your competitive advantage. What is it that sets your business above your competitors? Do you provide higher quality at competitive prices? Are you particularly good at customer service? Is your product or service unique? This kind of competitive advantage analysis sometime is hard for the owner of a business to perform, particularly if the owner has been with the business for a while. As a new owner, you should be able to do the analysis more easily. But if analytical skills are not your forte(, then this is time to retain a business consultant who is an expert in that area. This outsider's analysis and opinion can be valuable to you. (Please note that I have not recommended the use of consultants as a general rule in this book even though I am one! If you do need a consultant, hire one for a specific task and make sure the individual has expertise in the kind of work you want done.)

The next two steps are related to one another. To run a business profitably, you need some kind of cost accounting system. It can be fairly simple but should be reasonably accurate. Cost accounting systems can be quite tricky even in a small business, and if not designed properly, they can produce information that will lead you astray. The ultimate purpose of a cost accounting system is to let you know which products, services, or lines of business are profitable - and which ones aren't. This is the second part of this duo of turnaround steps: find out where you are making a profit and focus your efforts on those services or products. Sometimes less profitable business lines are maintained for customer service reasons, but as a turnaround specialist, you need to be hard-headed and hard-hearted. You need to chop off the items that are not making money or, even worse, the ones that are losers.

The last part of the plan is lowest priority but important in the long term: establish and maintain good relations with your banker, investors, industry group, chamber of commerce, community leaders, and other stakeholders. Communication is the key here. All of these people need to be informed as to what and how you are doing. In turn, you need to get information from them on developments in the financial world, industry, local economy, and community. Breakfasts, lunches, or short coffee breaks can be used to establish these relationships. This kind of networking gives you access to information and, more importantly, free advice. It also becomes important when you are ready to sell the business at a profit.

The Turnaround Action Plan

In a previous chapter, I discussed business and exit planning. Now comes the time to develop a turnaround plan. This is a much more detailed and specific action plan than either the business or exit plan.

Analysis of the financial statements showed you where to put most of your initial effort: increasing sales, decreasing direct or variable costs, or decreasing fixed costs. Then there are the practical "what do I do on Monday?" questions and answers. You have to face up to the fact that you have a limited amount of time and energy. You can't do everything. Now comes the time to prioritize and create an action plan.

This plan will be very specific, and you can lay it out in this format:

Step No.	Action	Resources Required			Time Req'd
		Hours	Dollars	Other	
1.					
2.					
3.					
4.					
5.					
etc.					

For example, step number one might be to perform a detailed review of fixed costs and list those items which need to be reduced. That becomes the "action." You figure it will take about 6 hours to accomplish that task and a period of two days. On the other hand, you may already have a pretty good idea as to what needs to be done in the way of reducing costs, so step one might be to contact three insurance agents for quotes on standard insurance for the business. You know it will take a total of 16 hours to contact the agents, meet with them, and get quotes. This process will probably take three weeks to complete.

Step number two then would be to contact ten key customers of the business to find out how they view the company and what they would like to see improved. You allocate five hours to this action, half an hour for each customer, and a time period of one week.

The turnaround action plan is built in this way. When it is completed, you will have a step-by-step plan to follow immediately after you take over as owner/manager. This will permit you to do the time management that is mandatory for any small business owner. Remember that some of your time will be spent "putting out fires," the ones that spontaneously ignite in any working day.

■

Chapter 13

THE TWO FASTEST TURNAROUNDS

Your goal is to make as much money as possible as fast as possible. In a previous chapter, I pointed out that your return - as a percentage - increases if you can generate the same amount of money in a shorter period of time. A gain of $100,000 on an investment of $100,000 represents a gain of 26% in three years - a good return - while it drops to just under 15% in five years, not much better than the stock market in a good three year period.

These rapid turnarounds depend absolutely and certainly on the naive owner, the one who believes that the balance sheet shows the value of the company. By the way, this is a very short chapter because these two kinds of deals don't require much explanation. You now know a lot about business turnarounds, and you should be able to understand the beauty of these situations without much detailed explanation.

A Cash-Flow versus Net Worth Imbalance

In this case, you did your homework and found out that, for some reason, the cash flow situation in the business provides a valuation that far exceeds the net worth on the balance sheet. This can happen for three reasons. One is vampire ownership, a situation described earlier in this book. The owner is sucking a lot of cash out of the business via insurance policies, travel expenses, or in other ways. Consequently there hasn't been much in the way of retained earnings and growth in net worth. Yet the owner is one of those people who looks at the net worth as the value of the company.

The other situation is one in which there has been a major shift upward in cash flow for the last year or two with some assurance that it will continue. This can happen for a variety of reasons. There may have been a turnover in personnel and the new team is much more productive. New ways of operating may have been introduced that resulted in a large drop in variable expenses. Or it could be as simple as the fact that the highest-margin product has begun selling at a faster rate while some lower margin items have dropped off.

Whatever the reason, the value of the business, based on projections of the cash flow, will be well above the book value on the balance sheet. If the situation were to continued very long, the book value would also begin to increase as long as the profits were retained in the company.

There is another possible reason for a reduced book value. Sometimes a company has to write off inventory or work in process. Some of the inventory may turn out to be "bad," or there may have been problems in inventory control resulting in an over-estimate of the stock actual available. In the case of work in process, the accounting system may have been unable to keep up with the work going out the door so that there was an over-statement of the work in process in the plant. If these situations occurred in the recent past, there probably was a sizable drop in the book value of the business.

The major effort in this situation is to re-cast the historical financial statements and to use them as a basis for a five year projection. The latter will show a dramatic increase in the net worth of the company or else show the real cash flow stream which can expected in the future. Those numbers become the basis for the prospectus you use in re-selling the company.

In all three of the situations described above, after you have purchased the business, re-cast the historical income statements and balance sheets to show what the company could have been worth had money been re-invested. You may have to make some assumptions on the effect of a re-investment in product or market development. You and your accountant can certainly show how the net worth would have increased had the cash flow simply been put into "retained earnings" each year.

More importantly, do projections for the next five years to show how the situation can be improved in a hurry and use this as the basis for your turnaround plan. The only thing you are doing here is taking the real cash flow of the business and showing the effect of re-investing it in the company will have on net worth.

Now here is the critical action: as soon as you have created the projections and turnaround plan, *immediately start looking for a buyer* and use your plan as the basis for your sales pitch. Here's the reason these are such fast turnarounds. They only involve a shift of numbers on paper. You don't even have to demonstrate that sales will or have increased, that efficiencies can be or have been accomplished. You simply do what the original owner should have done, which is put the financials in proper shape.

Under-Valued Real Estate (or Other Fixed Assets) on the Books

Now here is a situation that can be turned into profit faster than any other I have mentioned in this book. Unfortunately, this situation doesn't happen too often, but every once in a while it crops up. If it does, jump on it!

The situation is quite simple. A bookkeeper and accountant have kept the books for years with a company which owned its own building and land - real estate. Each year, the real estate was depreciated in accordance with the IRS rules. Each year the real estate probably *appreciates in value or at least stays the same.* So there is an increasingly large discrepancy between the value of the real estate on the books and in reality.

The owner, our classic naive owner, believes that the business is worth what it says on the balance sheet. This owner has no financial advisor. There is an accountant who is only called in to do the yearly taxes. A bookkeeper maintains the books, inserting the numbers the accountant comes up with each year. And the owner looks at the net worth of the business each year not realizing that the real value is probably far above what the books show.

The same situation can occur with any fixed assets in a business. However, most other fixed assets actually do depreciate. A computer controlled milling machine is worth less and less each year because of wear and tear as well as technological advances in the design of such equipment. High tech equipment such as computers, printers, digitizers, copiers, and so on depreciate very rapidly. Just check the prices for used computers that are only two or three years old! So your best bet is to look for cases where there is real estate involved.

If you ever find this kind of situation, make your offer in a hurry and hope that the owner doesn't consult a financial advisor or accountant before you sign on the dotted line. (Please note that this kind of deal is not likely to occur with a motel, restaurant, beauty salon, liquor store, or other enterprise brokered by a real estate firm. They are going to know the value of the land and building!) You will most often find a deal of this sort with a small manufacturing or technical operation or something similar.

After the purchase, your action plan is straightforward. Immediately strip the real estate out and get an appraisal of its current market value. Put the business up for sale with or without the land and building. If you sell the operating business without the real estate, you will have an income stream from the lease the new owner will sign with you. If you sell the real estate, you will have an immediate cash gain above what you paid for it. This is the closest thing to a slam-dunk opportunity for profit in buying and selling businesses.

■

Chapter 14

PREPARING FOR SALE

There are two aspects to preparing a business for sale. One is to operate it in such a way that it provides a good and increasing cash stream, and the other is to present the "story" of the business in an effective and appealing way. This is equivalent to having a good product plus a good sales pitch. For it, some people can get away with selling the heck out of a poor product. A few others manage to get customers to buy an excellent product without any sales efforts. But the best businesses involve an excellent product presented in an appealing way to customers. That is your job in preparing your business for sale.

If you follow the advice provided in the chapter of business planning and on performing the turnaround, your "product" - the business itself - should be in pretty good shape. You shouldn't have to do much more. I have provided a brief checklist below that you can use to make sure that all your bases are covered before you put the business up for sale. More of this chapter is devoted to putting together a good prospectus for the business. This prospectus becomes your sales tool when you approach potential buyers.

Preparations Checklist

For the naive seller, the first advice would be to recast the balance sheets and income statements for the last three to five years. You don't need that advice because you did it when you bought the business and should have continued to do so as you operated it. In addition, you probably have a good up-to-date set of records on the legal status of the business whether it be a corporation, partnership, or sole proprietorship. Again, people who have been running a business for a number of years often let these records slip, particularly Board and shareholder meeting agendas and minutes. You have maintained all those records.

The rest of your preparation ought to consist of the following items, none of which need much explanation:

1. List and update all contracts and agreements you have with customers, suppliers, the landlord, banks, and lenders.

2. List any trade secrets, patents, trademarks, and copyrights owned by the business (because these are "hidden" assets).

3. List all the insurance coverages on the business including normal business insurance, liability insurance, workers' compensation insurance, and any others; and summarize the coverages.

4. List all of the personnel in the company with titles and job descriptions and identify the people you consider to be key employees.

5. List all of the facilities and equipment with special emphasis on items which are unusual, unique, or otherwise provide a competitive advantage.

6. List data bases of customers, actual and potential, which again is a "hidden" asset not normally carried on the books.

7. Go through the company's files and make sure they are organized and neat.

8. Prepare for due diligence by a potential purchaser by making copies of key documents.

With those items taken care of, you have won half the battle.

The Prospectus

This is a sales document, one of the most important ones you will ever create because you are trying to maximize the money you will get for the business.

The prospectus should consist of the following:

Title Page

Non-Disclosure Agreement

Executive Summary

Financial Summary

    Net Worth

    Income Stream

    Owner Income

Legal Status

Business Plan

Existing Contracts and Agreements

Trade Secrets, Patents, Trademarks, and Copyrights

Insurance Coverage

Facilities and Equipment

Documentation

As you can see, the prospectus describes the various items mentioned in the preceding section of this chapter.

Most of the sections are self-explanatory, but a few words of description will help you understand what is needed. The title page should contain the word "Prospectus" and the name of the company. In addition, there should be a way to number each copy of the prospectus so that you can keep track of who gets them. Maintain a log so that you can write in the name of each party who have been given access to the document. A notice should be put on the title page to the effect that information contained in the prospectus is considered confidential, proprietary, and/or sensitive.

A non-disclosure agreement constitutes the second page. Consult your own attorney for the proper wording of the non-disclosure agreement. Every recipient should be asked to sign the agreement before being given a copy of the prospectus. If you want to really maintain tight security, seal the remaining pages of the document and do not allow the seal to be broken until the recipient has signed the agreement.

The potential buyer should see next a one page executive summary of the entire prospectus. Use one sentence to describe the company, its products or services, location, and legal form. Use another sentence to outline the current outlook for the business in terms of contracts, customers, market share, and business prospects. Summarize the financial condition by giving the net worth, net income, and value to the owner in terms of income. Provide a projection - based on the business plan which you have kept up to date - of the potential net worth and income stream for three to five years ahead. Finally, state the reason you want to sell.

Complete the executive summary with one sentence statements that summarize the personnel, insurance, coverage, facilities and equipment, documentation, and intellectual property rights of the company. Add any other information which will help sell the company to a prospective owner.

The executive summary should provide the reader with a complete but summarized picture of the business in a minute or two. It should tantalize the prospective purchaser into reading more of the prospectus.

Then go into detail in succeeding sections of the prospectus. Show a summary balance sheet and income state. Show the net worth and net profit trends over the last three to five years. If you have made a major improvement in the financial condition of the business, highlight it and explain how it happened. Did you increase sales? Decrease variable or fixed expenses? If so, provide graphs showing the changes over the three to five year period.

In the next section, discuss briefly the legal status of the business. If it is a corporation or partnership, list the other persons involved as shareholders, board members, or partners. If there are subsidiaries, list and describe them. If the business is a subsidiary, tell the reader the relationship of the business to the larger entity.

After the financial story is provided, the next most important part of the prospectus is a summary of the current business plan. (You can attach the complete business plan as an appendix to the prospectus.) The business plan tells the prospective owner what she or he can expect in the future not only based on financial results but also in terms of sales and marketing strategies, new product development, and similar matters. You should show what will be needed to sustain growth.

The remaining sections of the prospectus will be used to list and describe any existing contracts, agreements, or leases with particular emphasis on those which affect the valuation of the business. If you have a five year contract with a major customer that permits re-negotiation of pricing every six months, the new owner will have a cushion of sales for the next five years. If you have a favorable lease on the building occupied by the business, that should be highlighted. Of course, any contracts or agreements with potential negative impacts must also be included here.

This brings up an important point. The prospectus is a sales document, but it should also paint an accurate picture of the business. If there are problems, they need to be presented in a straightforward manner. Every business has problems. Everyone who has ever been around a small business knows that. Most buyers will appreciate honesty in this regard, and your prospectus will have greater credibility.

Put in at least a page describing the current personnel and discuss frankly how important they are to the continued growth of the company. If there are weak spots, describe them and what needs to be done to bolster the team in those areas.

Highlight any trade secrets, patents, trademarks, or copyrights the business holds. Tell the reader how long patents, trademarks, or copyrights will continue in effect and discuss developments and improvements that could result in new patents, trademarks, or copyrights.

Also list insurance coverages. This is important in letting the new owner know what has been covered and for how much in the past. In this same vein, be sure to disclose any claims pending on those insurance policies.

A paragraph or two or several pages can be devoted to facilities and equipment, particularly if they are important to the conduct of business. Finally, provide the prospective owner with some words on record keeping and documentation. Lack of paperwork and documentation can be a real potential hazard for the buyer, particularly if you do not intend to stick around during a transition period.

Again, remember that the prospectus is a sale document that should paint a positive but accurate picture of the status of the business. This means including some of the problems and how they can be solved. If the reader can believe the prospectus, your chances for getting a good offer are increased.

The key idea you should keep in mind is that selling a business is the same as selling anything else.

You need to do it actively. Just throwing the business out on the market won't do much good. The prospectus is the sale brochure for the business. It must present a solid case for why the company will make money for the next owner. After all, that is what a prospective owner is looking for. It is what you were looking for when you set out to buy a business.

■

Chapter 15

FINDING A BUYER

The time will come, of course, when you are ready to sell the business. You have done your work. There is increased profitability and cash flow. The net worth of the business has increased. It's time to find a buyer.

This is the reverse of the process of finding a business for sale but probably easier. There are a number of options. The most obvious is to use a business broker. This makes sense in several ways if you have increased the net worth and profitability enough to make it worthwhile. Business brokers have the contacts to find qualified buyers. The key here is the term "qualified." If you decide to sell the business on your own, you will also have to qualify each buyer, preferably before the process goes on too long. You don't want to sign an agreement in principle to sell and begin the due diligence process only to find out that the buyer can't raise the money.

A business broker will be a big help in finding a buyer fairly fast, particularly since you have done such a good job of turning the business around. That makes it salable. You have increased the chances of a quick sale by going through the process of preparing a prospectus as described in the last chapter.

Remember that time is your enemy in maximizing your return. The longer it takes to sell the business, the longer your money is tied up and the lower the return. *The biggest improvements in sales, cost control, and cash flow occur in the first year to three years so you need to sell at the end of or shortly after that time frame.* Continuing the turnaround and growth curve become more and more difficult with time. So pick the moment to sell carefully. Set the goals for profitability and net worth, and as you approach them, begin the process of finding a buyer.

The decision you have to make in retaining a business broker concerns the size of the commission versus the increase you have created in the worth of the company. For this, contact several brokers and ask them for their commission rates. Explain exactly what you are doing and why. In other words, tell these folks that you are in the business of buying and turning around small businesses. You know you have done the job on this particular business and are ready to sell, but you want to maximize your return. A good business broker will be more than happy to work with you. The obvious reason is that you will be a potential buyer after you sell this business. If the broker can create an effective relationship with you, there is money in his or her pocket for years to come.

You can also find a buyer on your own, and you have some potential allies in this endeavor. Get the word out. Have lunch with your banker. Explain what you are doing. Let her or him know that you are willing to sell to a qualified buyer. The banker has an inherent interest in seeing that the business continues to flourish under a new owner, and bankers have contacts throughout the community.

As with finding a business for sale, you should also tell your relatives, friends, and neighbors that you have a business available for sale. They can provide you with leads for potential buyers, particularly if they are involved in the business world.

Local chambers of commerce and economic development agencies can assist you in locating potential buyers as well. They will not act as agents or brokers, obviously, but they meet a lot of business people each working day. If they find someone who is looking to buy a business, the staff of these agencies can refer that person to you.

Generally, I would avoid listing the business in the want ads in the local papers. That may get you some contacts, but past experience suggests that most of them will not be qualified buyers.

Finally, do not overlook the possibility of selling the business to much larger corporation. Many big businesses are looking to acquire small businesses for several reasons. One is to acquire a technology, product, service, or process that can be used to enhance or supplement existing product lines. Another reason is to acquire a list of customers. Along those same lines, larger companies often make acquisitions to penetrate a new market area. Any easy way to do that is simply buy an existing business with its facilities, employees, and customer base.

To sell to a larger corporation, you will need to let them know that your business is available. There are directories that list the people in charge of corporate acquisitions in libraries. Business and professional associations also provide a means for getting that information.

As a final warning note in this chapter, I would think twice about contacting competitors as potential buyers or merger partners. This is particularly true if you and your competitors operate in a local or regional market. Mergers or acquisitions of competitor business in a local market - for example, hobby shops or machine shops - often don't work out.

The principal reason for recommending that you not solicit competitors is that they can come in and perform due diligence and then back out - with a great deal of information about your company. Even if you find a buyer, your competition will know more about your company than you or your successor knows about them.

There is one other possibility in selling a business. Sometimes it may make sense to sell off different products or business lines to different buyers. This can result in a larger overall return to you. So if the business has multiple business lines and particularly where those lines are in quite different industries, it may make sense to sell each line to a different acquirer.

■

Chapter 16

MOVING ON

What now? I would like to tell you that you probably made so much money on your first deal that you can retire. That isn't likely to happen.

You have made some money on this first turnaround venture. You certainly have learned a lot about the business world and yourself. At this point, you may still have some obligation as a consultant to the business you just sold.

In the process of buying and running the small business for a year or two or five, you have also developed a network of contacts in your bank, chamber of commerce, and community and with your customers and suppliers. Assuming you ran the business in a professional manner, you have created credibility as a business person. That is one of the most valuable assets you will carry with you.

If you enjoyed the process of turning around a small business and made some money, the logical thing to do is try again. You have an advantage here over the typical small business owner. You don't have a lot of ego invested in the business. You bought it in order to sell. Emotionally you should be ready to move on and try again.

Over a period of years, you can create wealth for yourself through the turnaround process. The other option you have is to buy another business and run it for a longer time period. Pay yourself well and enjoy being an owner and manager for a while. But when the time comes that you feel the enjoyment ebbing, be sure to get the business ready for sale in a timely fashion - long before you get sick of it and just want to bail out!

No matter which way you go, the world of small business ownership and management will hold many thrills for you - in addition to the downers. I wish you the best in your endeavors!

■

References and Bibliography

Buying and Selling Small Businesses

Berger, Lisa; Donelson Berger, and C. William Eastwood. *Ca$hing In: Getting the Most When You Sell Your Business.* New York: Warner Books, 1988.

Berget, Robert L. *12 Secrets to Cashing Out: How to Sell Your Company for the Most Profit.* Englewood Cliffs, N.J,: Prentice-Hall, 1994

Cox, Vaughn, *How to Sell your Business for the Best Price with the Least Worry.* Chicago: Probus Publishing, 1990.

Douglas, F. Gordon. *How to Profitably Sell or Buy a Company or Business.* New York: Van Nostrand Rheinhold, 1981.

Peterson, C. D. *How to Leave Your Job & Buy a Business of Your Own.* New York: McGraw-Hill. 1988.

Sperry, Paul S. and Beatrice H. Mitchell. *The Complete Guide to Selling Your Business.* Dover, New Hampshire: Upstart Publishing, 1992.

Bankruptcies

Kallen, Laurence H. *How to Get Rich Buying Bankrupt Companies.* New York: Carol Communications, 1992

Levine, Sumner N. *Investing in Bankrupticies & Turnarounds: Spotting Investment Values in Distressed Businesses.* New York: HarperCollins, 1991.

The Sourcebook of Federal Courts: U.S. District and Bankruptcy. BRB Publications Inc.

Business Planning

Rich, Stanley R. and David E. Gumpert. *Business Plans that Win $$$*. New York: Harper & Row, 1985.

Dible, Donald M. (Editor). *How to Plan and Finance a Growing Business*. Fairfield, CA: The Entrepreneur Press, 1980.

Valuing a Business

Martin, Thomas J. *Valuation Reference Manual*. Hicksville, N.Y.: Thomas Publications, 1987.

McCarthy, George D. and Robert E. Healy. *Valuing a Company: Practices and Procedures*. New York: John Wiley & Sons, 1971.

Pratt, Shannon. *Valuing a Business: The Analysis and Appraisal of Closely-Held Companies*. Homewood, Illinois: Dow Jone-Irwin, 1981.

Mergers and Acquisitions

Joseph H Marren. *Mergers & Acquisitions: Will You Overpay?* Homewood, IL: Dow Jones-Irwin 1985

Finance and Accounting Basics

Droms, William S. *Finance and Accounting for Nonfinancial Managers*. Reading, Massachusetts: Addison-Wesley, 1983.

Woelfel, Charles J. *Financial Statement Analysis*. Chicago: Probus Publishing, 1988.

Shim, Jae K. and Joel G. Siegel. *Handbook of Financial Analysis, Forecasting, and Modeling*. Englewood Cliffs, N.J.: Prentice Hall, 1988.

Financing a Business

Lindsey, Jennifer. *Start-Up Money: Raise What You Need for Your Small Business*. New York: John Wiley & Sons, 1989.

Mancuso, Joseph R. *How to Get a Business Loan (Without Signing Your Life Away)*. New York: Simon & Schuster, 1990.

Postyn, Sol and Jo Kirschner Postyn. *Raising Cash: A Guide to Financing and Controlling Your Business*. Belmont, CA: Lifetime Learning Publications, 1982.

Silver, A. David. Venture Capital: *The Complete Guide for Investors*. New York: John Wiley & Sons, 1985.
References and Bibliography

Appendix A

Small Business Administration Field Offices

Note: The SBA offices change locations and phone numbers at times. This list shows you where offices are located. Check your local phone book in the section with governmental listings.

Alabama
Birmingham

Alaska
Anchorage
Fairbanks

Arizona
Phoenix
Tucson

Arkansas
Little Rock

California.
Fresno
Los Angeles
Oakland
Sacramento
San Diego
San Francisco
Santa Ana

Colorado
Denver

Connecticut
Hartford

Delaware
Wilmington

District of Columbia
Washington

Florida
Jacksonville
Coral Gables
Tampa
West Palm Beach

Georgia
Atlanta
Stateboro

Guam
Agena

Hawaii
Honolulu

Idaho
Boise

Illinois
Chicago
Springfield

Indiana
South Bend
Indianapolis

Iowa
Des Moines
Cedar Rapids

Kansas
Wichita

Kentucky
Louisville

Louisiana
New Orleans
Shreveport

Maine
Augusta

Maryland
Towson

Massachusetts
Boston
Holyoke

Michigan
Detroit

Minnesota
Minneapolis

Mississippi
Biloxi
Jackson

Missouri
Kansas City
Sikeston
Springfield

Montana
Helena

Nebraska
Omaha

New Jersey
Camden
Newark

New Mexico
Albuquerque

New York
Albany
Buffalo
Elmira
Melville
New York
Rochester
Syracuse

North Carolina
Charlotte
Greenville

North Dakota
Fargo

Ohio
Cleveland
Columbus
Cincinnati

Oklahoma
Oklahoma City
Tulsa

Oregon
Portland

Pennsylvania
Bala Cynwyd
Harrisburg
Pittsburgh
Wilkes-Barre

Puerto Rico
Hato Rey

Rhode Island
Providence

South Carolina
Columbia

South Dakota
Sioux Falls

Tennessee
Knoxville
Memphis
Nashville

Texas
Austin
Corpus Christi
Dallas
El Paso
Harlingen
Houston

Lubbock
Marshall
San Antonio

Utah
Salt Lake City

Vermont
Montpelier

Virginia
Richmond

Virgin Islands
St. Thomas

Washington
Seattle
Spokane

West Virginia
Clarksburg
Charleston

Wisconsin
Eau Claire
Madison
Milwaukee

Wyoming
Casper

Appendix B

Federal Bankruptcy Courts

Federal bankruptcy courts are organized by districts and divisions. Some states have more than one district and may have more than one division in each district. Less populous states constitute a district and have only one division. In all cases, the district is listed first and division second in this appendix. Also, the main court is indicated by an * for each district and/or division.

Alabama
Middle District
  Montgomery
Northern District
  Anniston
  Montgomery*
  Decatur
  Tuscaloosa
Southern District
  Mobile

Alaska
Anchorage

Arizona
Phoenix*
Tucson
Yuma

Arkansas
Eastern District
  Little Rock
Western District
  Fayetteville

California
Central District
  Santa Ana
  Santa Barbara
  San Bernardino
  Los Angeles*
Northern District
  Oakland
  San Francisco*
  San Jose
  Santa Rosa
Eastern District
  Fresno
  Modesto
  Sacramento*
Southern District
  San Diego

Colorado
Denver

Connecticut
Bridgeport
Hartford*

Delaware
Wilmington

District of Columbia
Washington

Florida
Middle District
  Jacksonville
  Orlando
  Tampa*
Northern District
  Pensacola
  Tallahassee*
Southern District
  Fort Lauderdale
  Miami*

Georgia
Middle District
  Columbus
  Macon*
Northern District
  Atlanta*
  Gainesville

Newman
Rome
Southern District
  Augusta*
  Savannah

Hawaii
Honolulu

Idaho
Boise*
Moscow
Pocatello
Coeur d'Alene

Illinois
Central District
  Danville
  Peoria
  Springfield*
Northern District
  Chicago*
  Rockford
Southern District
  Benton
  East St. Louis*

Indiana
Northern District
  Ft. Wayne
  Hammond at
    Gary
  Hammond at
    Lafayette
  South Bend*
Southern District
  Evansville
  Indianapolis*
  New Albany
  Terre Haute

Iowa
Northern District
  Cedar Rapids
Southern District
  Des Moines

Kansas
Kansas City
Topeka
Wichita*

Kentucky
Eastern District
  Lexington
Western District
  Louisville

Louisiana
Eastern District
  New Orleans
Middle District
  Baton Rouge
Western District
  Alexandria
  Lafayette
  Opelousas
  Monroe
  Shreveport*
  Lake Charles

Maine
Bangor
Portland*

Maryland
Baltimore*
Rockville

Massachusetts
Boston*
Worcester

Michigan
Eastern District
  Bay City
  Detroit*
  Flint
Western District
  Southern Division
    Grand Rapids*
  Northern Division
    Marquette

Minnesota
Duluth
Fergus Falls
Minneapolis
St. Paul

Mississippi
Northern District
  Aberdeen,
  Eastern Division
Southern District
  Jackson Division

Missouri
Eastern District
  St. Louis Division
Western District
  Kansas City,
  Western Division

Montana
Butte

Nebraska
Lincoln
North Platte
  (search at
  Omaha Div.)
Omaha*

Nevada
Las Vegas
Reno

New Hampshire
Manchester

New Jersey
Camden
Newark
Trenton*

New Mexico
Albuquerque

New York
Eastern District
  Brooklyn*
  Hauppauge
  Westbury
Southern District
  New York*
  Poughkeepsie
  White Plains
Northern
  Albany*
  Utica
Western
  Buffalo*
  Rochester

North Carolina
Eastern District
  Raleigh
  Wilson*
Middle District
  Greensboro
Western District
  Charlottte

North Dakota
Fargo

Ohio
Northern District
  Akron
  Canton
  Cleveland*
  Toledo
  Youngstown
Southern
  Cincinnati*
  Columbus
  Dayton

Oklahoma
Eastern District
  Okmulgee
Northern District
  Tulsa
Western District
  Oklahoma City

Oregon
Eugene
Portland*

Pennsylvania
Eastern District
  Philadelphia*
  Reading
Middle District
  Harrisburg
  Wilkes-Barre
Western District
  Erie
  Pittsburgh*

Rhode Island
Providence

South Carolina
Columbia

South Dakota
Pierre
Sioux Falls*

Tennessee
Eastern District
  Chattanooga
  Knoxville*
Middle District
  Nashville
Western District
  Jackson
  Memphis*

Texas
Eastern District
  Beaumont
  Lufkin
  Marshall
  Plano
  Texarkana
  Tyler
  (Note: Beaumont handles all filing for Marshall, Lufkin, and Texarkana)
Southern District
  Corpus Christi
  Houston*
Northern District
  Amarillo
  Dallas*
  Fort Worth
  Lubbock
  Wichita Falls
Western District
  Austin
  Del Rio
  El Paso
  Midland/Odessa
  Pecos
  San Antonio*
  Waco

Utah
Salt Lake City
(Note: Cases are divided
into northern and central
divisions.)

Vermont
Rutland

Virginia
Eastern District
    Alexandria
    Newport News
    Norfolk
    Richmond*
Western District
    Harrisburg
    Lynchburg
    Roanoke

Washington
Eastern District
    Spokane
Western District
    Seattle*
    Tacoma

West Virginia
Northern District
    Wheeling
Southern District
    Charleston

Wisconsin
Eastern District
    Milwaukee
Western District
    Eau Claire
    Madison*

Wyoming
Cheyenne

Appendix C

State Development Agencies

Alabama
Alabama Development Office
c/o State Capitol
Montgomery, AL 36130

Alaska
Alaska Department of
  Commerce and Economic
  Development
Division of Economic
  Enterprise
Pouch EE
Juneau, AK 99811

Arizona
Arizona Office of Economic
  Planning & Development
17 West Washington
Phoenix, AZ 85007

Arkansas
Arkansas Industrial
  Development Commission
State Capitol
Little Rock, AR 72201

California
California Department of
  Economic & Business
  Development
Office of Business &
  Industrial Development
1120 N St.
Sacramento, CA 95814

Colorado
Colorado Division of
  Commerce & Development
1313 Sherman St., Room 500
Denver, CO 80203

Connecticut
Connecticut Department
  of Commerce
210 Washington St.
Hartford, CT 06106

Delaware
Delaware Department of
  Community Affairs &
  Economic Development
Division of Economic
  Development
630 State College Rd.
Dover, DE 19901

Florida
Florida Department of
  Commerce
Division of Economic
  Development
Collins Building
Tallahassee, FL 32304

Georgia
Georgia Department of
  Industry & Trade
Post Office Box 1776
Atlanta, GA 30301

Hawaii
Hawaii Department of
  Planning & Economic
  Development
Post Office Box 2359
Honolulu, HI 96804

Idaho
Idaho Division of Tourism &
  Industrial Development
State Capitol Building,
Room 108
Boise, ID 83720

Illinois
Illinois Department of
  Business & Economic
  Development
222 South College St.
Springfield, IL 62706

Indiana
Indiana Department of
  Commerce
1350 Consolidate Building
115 North Pennsylvania St.
Indianapolis, IN 46204

Iowa
Iowa Development
  Commission
250 Jewett Building
Des Moines, IA 50309

Kansas
Kansas Department of
  Economic Development
503 Kansas Ave.
Topeka, KS 66603

Kentucky
Kentucky Department of
  Commerce
Capitol Plaza Office Tower
Frankfort, KY 40601

Louisiana
Louisiana Department of
  Commerce & Industry
Post Office Box 44185
Baton Rouge, LA 70804

Maine
Main State Development
  Office
Executive Department
  State House
Augusta, ME 04333

Maryland
Maryland Department of
Economic & Community
  Development
2525 Riva Rd.
Annapolis, MD 21401

Massachusetts
Massachusetts Department of
  Commerce & Development
100 Cambridge St.
Boston, MA 02202

Michigan
Michigan Department of
  Commerce
Office of Economic
  Expansion
Post Office Box 30225
Lansing, MI 48909

Minnesota
Minnesota Department of
  Economic Development
480 Cedar Street
St. Paul, MN 55101

Mississippi
Mississippi Agricultural &
  Industrial Board
Post Office Box 849
Jackson, MS 39205

Missouri
Missouri Division of
  Commerce & Industrial
  Development
Post Office Box 118
Jefferson City, MO 65101

Montana
Montana Department of
  Community Affairs
Economic Development
  Division
Capitol Station
Helena, MT 59601

Nebraska
Nebraska Department of
  Economic Development
Box 94666 - State Capitol
Lincoln, NE 68509

Nevada
Nevada Department of
  Economic Development
Capitol Complex
Carson City, NV 89710

New Hampshire
New Hampshire Office of
  Industrial Development
Division of Economic
  Development
Department of Resources &
  Economic Development
Post Office Box 856
Concord, NH 03301

New Jersey
New Jersey Department of
  Labor & Industry
Division of Economic
  Development
Post Office Box 2766
Trenton, NJ 08625

New Mexico
New Mexico Department
  of Development
113 Washington Ave
Santa Fe, NM 87503

New York
New York State Department
  of Commerce
99 Washington Ave.
Albany, NY 12245

North Carolina
North Carolina Department
  of Natural and Economic
  Development
Division of Economic
  Development
Box 27687
Raleigh, NC 27611

North Dakota
North Dakota Business and
Industrial Development
  Department
523 East Bismarck Ave.
Bismarck, ND 58505

Ohio
Ohio Department of
  Economic and Community
  Development
Box 1001
Columbus, OH 43216

Oklahoma
Oklahoma Department of
  Industrial Development
600 Will Rogers Building
Oklahoma City, OK 73105

Oregon
Oregon Department of
  Economic Development
317 South West Alder St.
Portland, OR 97204

Pennsylvania
Pennsylvania Department
  of Commerce
Division of Research &
  Planning
632 Health and Welfare Bldg.
Harrisburg, PA 17120

Rhode Island
Rhode Island Department of
  Economic Development
One Weybosset Hill
Providence, RI 02903

South Carolina
South Carolina State
  Development Board
Post Office Box 927
Columbia, SC 29202

South Dakota
South Dakota Department
  of Economic & Tourism
  Development
620 South Cliff
Sioux Falls, SD 57103

Tennessee
Tennessee Department of
  Economic & Community
  Development
1014 Andrew Jackson State
  Office Building
Nashville, TN 37219

Texas
Texas Industrial Commission
714 Sam Houston State
  Office Building
Austin, TX 78711

Utah
Utah Department of
  Development Services
No. 2 Arrow Press Square,
  Suite 200
165 South West Temple
Salt Lake City, UT 84101

Vermont

Vermont Agency of
Development &
   Community Affairs
Economic Development
   Department
Pavilion Office Building
Montpelier, VT 05602

Virginia

Virginia Division of
   Industrial Development
1010 State Office Building
Richmond, VA 23219

Washington

Washington State Department
   of Commerce &
   Economic Development
101 General Administration
   Building
Olympia, WA 98504

West Virginia

West Virginia Department
   of Commerce
Industrial Development
   Division
1900 Washington St. East
Charleston, WV 25305

Wisconsin

Wisconsin Department of
   Business Development
123 West Washington
Madison, WI 53702

Wyoming

Wyoming Department of
   Economic Planning &
   Development
Barrett Building, Third Floor
Cheyenne, WY 82002

Appendix D

Small Business Development Centers

Each state has a network of Small Business Development Centers, most associated with colleges and universities. The following list provides the State Director location and phone number and then the institutions and cities for the local SBDCs. To contact a local SBDC office call the State Director's office for a phone number and address or else look up the office in the local phone book.

Alabama
State Director
University of Alabama at
    Birmingham SBDC
Medical Towers Bldg
1717 11th Ave. South, Suite 419
Birmingham, AL 35294-4410
(205) 934-7260
    Auburn
    Birmingham
    Florence
    Huntsville
    Jacksonville
    Livingston
    Mobile
    Montgomery
    Troy
    Tuscaloosa

Alaska
State Director
University of Alaska
    Anchorage
430 W. Seventh St. Suite 110
Anchorage, AK 99501
    Anchorage
    Fairbanks
    Juneau
    Wasilla

Arizona
State Director
Arizona SBDC Network
9215 N. Canyon Highway
Phoenix, AZ 85021
    Holbrook
    Lake Havasu City
    Phoenix
    Prescott
    Sacaton
    Safford
    Sierra Vista
    Tucson
    Yuma

Arkansas
State Director
Univ. of Arkansas at Little
Rock
100 S. Main, Suite 401
Little Rock, AR 72201
(501) 324-9043
  Arkadelphia
  Batesville
  Beebe
  Conway
  Fayetteville
  Helena
  Jonesboro
  Monticello
  Searcy

California
State Director
Small Business
  Development Center
801 K St., 17th Floor,
Suite 1700
Sacramento, CA 95814
(916) 324-5068
  Aptos
  Auburn
  Bakersfield
  Chico
  Chula Vista
  Crescent City
  Eureka
  Fresno
  Gilroy
  Lakeport
  La Jolla
  Los Angeles
  Merced
  Modesto
  Napa
  Riverside
  Oakland

Oxnard
Pomona
Merced
Modesto
Sacramento
San Jose
San Mateo
Santa Ana

Colorado
State Director
Small Business
  Development Center
Office of Business Development
1625 Broadway, Suite 1710
Denver, CO 80202
(303) 892-3809
  Alamosa
  Aurora
  Canon City
  Colorado Springs
  Craig
  Delta
  Denver
  Durango
  Fort Collins
  Fort Morgan
  Grand Junction
  Greeley
  Lakewood
  Lamar
  Littleton
  Pueblo
  Stratton
  Trinidad
  Vail
  Westminster

Connecticut
State Director
Small Business
   Development Center
Univ. of Connecticut
Box U-41, Rm. 422
368 Fairfield Rd.
Storrs, CT 06269-2041
(203) 486-4135
   Bridgeport
   Groton
   Middletown
   New Haven
   Stamford
   Storrs
   Waterbury
   West Hartford
   Willimantic

Delaware
State Director
University of Delaware
Purnell Hall, Suite 005
Newark, DE 19716-2711

District of Columbia
State Director
Small Business
   Development Network
Howard University
2600 Sixth St, Room #128
Washington, DC 20059
   Landover, MD
   Washington, DC

Florida
State Director
Florida SBDC Network
University of Florida
Bldg. 76, Rm. 231
Pensacola, FL 32514
   Boca Raton
   Dania
   Deland
   Fort Myers
   Ft. Pierce
   Fort Walton Beach
   Gainesville
   Jacksonville
   Miami
   Orlando
   Palm Beach Gardens
   Panama City
   Pensacola
   St. Petersburg
   Sarasota
   Tallahassee
   Tampa

Georgia
State Director
Small Business
   Development Center
Univ. of Georgia,
Chicopee Complex
1180 East Broad St.
Athens, GA 30602
(404) 542-5760
   Albany
   Athens
   Atlanta
   Brunswick
   Columbus
   Decatur
   Gainesville
   Lawrenceville
   Macon

Marietta
Morrow
Rome
Savannah
Statesboro

Hawaii
State Director
Hawaii SBDC Network
University of Hawaii at Hilo
523 W. Lanikaula St.
Hilo, HI 96720-4091
(808) 933-3515
   Hilo
   Lihue
   Kahului

Idaho
State Director
Small Business
   Development Center
Boise State Univ.
1910 University Drive
Boise, ID 83725
(208) 385-1640
   Boise
   Hayden
   Idaho Falls
   Lewiston
   Pocatello
   Sandpoint
   Twin Falls

Illinois
Statewide Administrator
Small Business
   Development Center
Dept. of Commerce &
   Comm. Affairs
620 East Adams St., 6th Floor
Springfield, IL 62701
(217) 524-5856

Aledo
Aurora
Bloomington
Canton
Carbondale
Centralia
Champaign
Chicago (18 locations)
Danville
Decatur
Dekalb
Dixon
Edwardsville
Elgin
Evanston
Geneseo
Glen Ellyn
Grayslake
Ina
Joliet
Kewanee
Macomb
Mattoon
Melrose Park
Moline
Monmouth
Oglesby
Palos Hills
Peoria
Quincy
Rockford
Springfield
Ullin
University Park

Indiana
Executive Director
Indiana SBDC
One North Capitol, Suite 420
Indianapolis, IN 46204
(317) 264-6871
   Bloomington

Columbus
Evansville
Fort Wayne
Gary
Jeffersonville
Indianapolis
Kokomo
Lafayette
Laporte
Merrillville
Munie
Richmond
South Bend
Terre Haute

Iowa
State Director
Iowa SBDC
Iowa State Univ., 137 Lynn Ave.
Ames, IA 50010
(515) 292-6351
   Ames
   Audobon
   Cedar Falls
   Council Bluffs
   Creston
   Davenport
   Des Moines
   Dubuque
   Iowa City
   Marion
   Mason City
   Ottumwa
   Sioux City
   Spencer
   West Burlington

Kansas
Director
Wichita State Univ.
1845 Fairmont,
Campus Box 148

Wichita, KS 67208
(316) 689-3193
   Arkansas City
   Augusta
   Colby
   Dodge City
   Emporia
   Garden City
   Great Bend
   Hutchinson
   Hays
   Kansas City
   Lawrence
   Liberal
   Manhattan
   Ottawa
   Overland Park
   Pittsburg
   Pratt
   Salina
   Topeka
   Wichita

Kentucky
State Director
University of Kentucky
225 Business and
   Economics Bldg.
Lexington, KY 40506-0034
   Ashland
   Bowling Green
   Cumberland
   Elizabethtown
   Highland Heights
   Hopkinsville
   Lexington
   Louisville
   Morehead
   Murray
   Owensboro
   Pikeville
   Somerset

Louisiana
State Director
Northeast Louisiana Univ.
Adm. 2-57
Monroe, LA 71209-6435
  Baton Rouge
  Hammond
  Lafayette
  Monroe
  Natchitoches
  New Orleans (4)
  Ruston
  Shreveport
  Thibodaux

Maine
Director
University of Southern Maine
96 Falmouth St.
Portland, ME 04103
(207) 780-4420
  Auburn
  Bangor
  Caribou
  Machias
  Sanford
  Winslow
  Wiscasset

Maryland
Director
State Administrative Office
Dept. of Economic &
  Employment Development
217 East Redwood St.,
10th Floor
Baltimore, MD 21202
(410) 333-6996
  Baltimore
  Bethesda
  Cumberland
  Landover

  Salisbury
  Waldorf

Massachusetts
State Director
MSBDC Network, State Office
University of Massachusetts
School of Management,
Rm 205
Amherst, MA 01003
(413) 545-6301
  Boston
  Chestnut Hill (2)
  Fall River
  Springfield
  Worcester
  Salem

Michigan
State Director
Michigan SBDC
2727 Second Ave.
Detroit, MI 48201
(313) 577-4848
  Allendale
  Ann Arbor
  Bad Axe
  Battle Creek
  Benton Harbor
  Kalamazoo
  Big Rapids
  Cadillac
  Caro
  Detroit (3)
  East Lansing
  Escanaba
  Flint
  Grand Rapids
  Hart
  Grand Rapids
  Hart
  Houghton (2)

Howell
Lansing
Lapeer
Kalamazoo
Marlette
Marquette
Mt. Pleasant
Muskegon
Peck
Port Huron
Saginas
Scottville
Sidney
Sterling Heights (2)
Traverse City (4)
Troy
University Center

Minnesota

State Director
Small Business
    Development Center
Dept. of Trade and
    Economic Devel.
900 American Center Bldg.
150 East Kellogg Blvd.
St. Paul, MN 55101
(612) 297-5770
    Bemidji
    Bloomington
    Brainerd
    Duluth
    Faribault
    Grand Rapids
    Hibbing
    International Falls
    Mankato
    Marshall
    Minneapolis
    Moorhead
    Pine City
    Plymouth

Red Wing
Rochester
Rosemount
St. Cloud
St. Paul
Thief River Falls
Virginia
Wadena
White Bear Lake
Winona

Mississippi

Executive Director
Small Business
    Development Center
Old Chemistry Bldg.
Suite 216
University, MS 38677
(601) 232 5001
    Cleveland
    Greenville
    Hattiesburg
    Jackson (2)
    Long Beach
    Meridian
    Mississippi State
    Natchez
    Tupelo
    Vicksburg

Missouri

State Directors
MO SBDC (State Office)
University of Missouri
300 University Place
Columbia, MO 65211
(314) 882 0344
    Cape Girardeau
    Columbia
    Flat River
    Jefferson City (2)
    Joplin

Kansas City
Kirksville
Maryville
Poplar Bluff
Rolla (2)
St. Joseph
St. Louis
Springfield
Warrensburg

Montana
State Director
Helena SBDC
1424 Ninth Ave.
Helena, MT 59620
(406) 444-4780
   Billings
   Bozeman
   Butte
   Havre
   Kalispell
   Missoula
   Sidney

Nebraska
State Director
NBDC - Omaha
University of Nebraska
   at Omaha
60th & Dodge Street
CBA, Room 407
Omaha, NE 68182
(402) 554-2521
   Chadron
   Kearney
   Lincoln
   North Platte
   Omaha
   Peru
   Scottsbluff
   Wayne

Nevada
State Director
Small Business
   Development Center
University of Nevada, Reno
College of Business
   Administration-032
Room 411
Reno, NV 89557-0100
(702) 784-1717
   Elko
   Las Vegas

New Hampshire
State Director, SBDC
University of New Hampshire
108 McConnell Hall
Durham, NH 03824
(603) 862-2200
   Durham (2)
   Keene
   Littleton
   Manchester
   Nashua
   Plymouth

New Jersey
State Director
Small Business
   Development Center
Rutgers University
180 University Ave.
3rd Floor - Ackerson Hall
Newark, NJ 07102
(201) 648-5950
   Atlantic City
   Camden
   Lincroft
   Newark
   Trenton
   Union
   Washington

New Mexico
State Director
NMSBDC Lead Center
Santa Fe Community College
P.O. Box 4187
Santa Fe, NM 87502-4187
(505) 438-1362
　Alamogordo
　Albuquerque
　Carlsbad
　Clovis
　Espanola
　Farmington
　Gallup
　Grants
　Hobbs
　Las Cruces
　Las Vegas
　Los Alamos
　Los Lunas
　Roswell
　Santa Fe
　Silver City
　Tucumcari

New York
State Director
Small Business
　Development Center
State Univ. of New York
SUNY Central Plaza S-523
Albany, NY 12246
(518) 443-5398
　Albany
　Binghamton
　Brooklyn
　Buffalo
　Corning
　Farmingdale
　Jamaica
　Jamestown
　New York
　Plattsburgh
　Riverdale
　Rochester
　Sanborn
　Stony Brook
　Stone Ridge
　Suffern
　Syracuse
　Utica
　Watertown

North Carolina
Executive Director
NC SBDC Headquarters Office
Univ. of N. Carolina at
　Chapel Hill
4509 Creedmor Rd., Suite 201
Raleigh, NC 27612
1-800-2580-UNC
　Boone
　Charlotte
　Cullowhee
　Elizabeth City
　Fayetteville
　Greenville
　Greensboro
　Raleigh
　Wilmington
　Winston-Salem

North Dakota
State Director
State Center/Grank Forks
118 Gamble Hall, UND
Box 7308
Grank Forks, ND 58202-7308
(701) 777-3700
　Bismark
　Dickinson
　Grand Forks
　Fargo
　Minot

Ohio
State Director
Small Business
  Development Center
77 South High St.
P.O. Box 1001
Columbus, OH 43226
(614) 466-2711
  Akron (2)
  Archbold
  Bellefontaine
  Canton
  Cambridge
  Celina
  Cincinnati
  Cleveland
  Columbus
  Dayton
  Freemont
  Hillsboro
  Jefferson
  Lima
  Lorain
  Mansfield
  Oxford
  Piqua
  St. Clairsville
  Sandusky
  Southpoint
  Steubenville
  Toledo
  Youngstown
  Zanesville

Oklahoma
State Director
Small Business
  Development Center
Southeastern Oklahoma Univ.
Station A, Box 2584
Durant, OK 74701
(405) 924-0277

  Ada
  Alva
  Durant
  Edmond
  Enid
  Langston
  Lawton
  Midwest City
  Muskogee
  Oklahoma City
  Poteau
  Tehlequah
  Tulsa
  Weatherford

Oregon
State Director
Small Business
  Development Center
Lane Community College
99 W. 10th, Suite 216
Eugene, OR 97401
(503) 726-2250
  Albany
  Ashland
  Bend
  Coos Bay
  The Dalles
  Eugene
  Grants Pass
  Gresham
  Klamath Falls
  Lincoln
  Medford
  Milwaukee
  Ontario
  Pendleton
  Portland (2)
  Roseburg
  Salem
  Seaside
  Tillamook

Pennsylvania
State Director
Small Business
   Development Center
University of Pennsylvania
The Wharton School, 444
Vance Hall
Philadelphia, PA 19104
(215) 898-1219
   Bethlehem
   Clarion
   Erie
   Latrobe
   Lewisburg
   Loretto
   Middletown
   Philadelphia (2)
   Pittsburgh (2)
   Scranton
   Wilkes-Barre

Puerto Rico
State Director
Small Business
   Development Center
University of Puerto Rico
P.O. Box 5253 College Station
Mayaguez, PR 00681
(809) 834-3590
   Hato Rey
   Humacao
   Mayaguez
   Ponce
   Rio Piedres

Rhode Island
State Director
State Administrative Office
Bryant College RISBDC
1150 Douglas Pike
Smithfield, RI 02917
   Kingston

Middletown
Providence (2)
Smithfield

South Carolina
State Director
Small Business
   Development Center
Univ. of S. Carolina, 1710
Coll. St.
Columbia, SC 29208
(803) 777-4907
   Beaufort
   Charleston
   Clemson
   Columbia (2)
   Conway
   Greenville
   Florence
   Greenwood
   North Augusta
   Orangeburg
   Rock Hill (2)
   Spartanburg

South Dakota
State Director
Small Business
   Development Center
University of South Dakota
414 East Clark
Vermillion, SD 57069
(605) 677-5272
   Aberdeen
   Pierre
   Rapid City (2)
   Sioux Falls
   Vermillion

Tennessee
State Director
Small Business
    Development Center
Memphis State University
Bldg. 1, South Campus
Memphis, TN 38152
(901) 678-2500
    Chattanooga
    Clarksville
    Cleveland
    Cookeville
    Dyersburg
    Jackson
    Johnson City
    Knoxville
    Martin
    Memphis
    Morristown
    Murfreesboro
    Nashville

Texas-Dallas
Region Director
North Texas-Dallas SBDC
Bill J. Priest Institute for
    Economic Development
1402 Corinth St.
Dallas, TX 75215
(214) 565-5833
    Athens
    Bonham
    Corsicana
    Dallas (3)
    Denison
    Denton
    DeSoto
    Ft. Worth
    Gainesville
    Hillsboro
    Longview
    Mt. Pleasant

    Paris
    Plano
    Tyler
    Waco

Texas-Houston
Regional Director
Small Business
    Development Center
University of Houston
601 Jefferson, Suite 2330
Houston, TX 77002
(713) 752-8444
    Alvin
    Baytown
    Beaumont
    Brenham
    Bryan
    Galveston
    Houston (4)
    Hunstville
    Kingwood
    Lake Jackson
    Lufkin
    Stafford
    Texas City
    Wharton

Texas-Lubbock
Region Director
Northwest Texas SBDC
2579 South Loop 289,
Suite 114
Lubbock, TX 79423
(806) 745-3973
    Abilene
    Amarillo
    Lubbock
    Odessa
    Stephensville
    Wichita Falls

Texas-San Antonio
Regional Director
UTSA South Texas
   Border SBDC
UTSA Downtown Center
801 S. Bowie Street
San Antonio, TX 78205
(512) 224-0791
   Austin
   Corpus Christi
   Edinburg
   El Paso
   Kingsville
   Laredo
   San Angelo
   San Antonio (2)
   Uvalde
   Victoria

Utah
State Director
Small Business
   Development Center
University of Utah
102 West 500 South, Suite 315
Salt Lake City, UT 84101
(801) 581-7905
   Cedar City
   Ephraim
   Logan
   Ogden
   Price
   Provo
   St. George

Vermont
State Director
Vermont SBDC
1 Blair Park
Suite 13
Williston, VT 054950-9404
(802) 878-0181
   Brattleboro
   Colchester
   Montpelier
   Rutland
   St. Johnsbury

Virginia
State Director
Virginia SBDC
P.O. Box 798,
1021 East Cary St.
11 Floor
Richmond, VA 23219
(804) 371-8258
   Arlington
   Big Stone Gap
   Blacksburg
   Charlottesville
   Farmville
   Fairfax
   Harrisonburg
   Lynchburg
   Manassas
   Norfolk
   Radford
   Richlands
   Richmond (2)
   Roanoke
   South Bostom
   Sterling
   Wytheville

Virgin Islands
State Director
Small Business
   Development Center
University of the Virgin Islands
Grand Hotel Building,
Annex B
P.O. Box 1087
St. Thomas, VI 00804
(809) 776-3206
   St. Croix

Washington
State Director
Small Business Development
Center
Washington State Univ.
245 Todd Hall
Pullman, WA 99164-4727
(509) 335-1576
   Bellevue
   Bellingham
   Centralia
   Everett
   Kennewick
   Moses Lake
   Mt. Vernon
   Olympia (2)
   Omok
   Seattle (3)
   Spokane
   Tacoma
   Vancouver
   Wenatchee
   Yakima

West Virginia
State Director
Small Business
   Development Center
Governor's Office of Comm.
   & Ind.
1115 Virginia Street
East Capitol Complex
Charleston, WV 25301
(304) 348-2960
   Athens
   Bluefield
   Charleston
   Fairmont
   Huntington
   Keyser
   Montgomery
   Morgantown
   Parkersburg
   Shepherdstown
   Wheeling

Wisconsin
State Director
Small Business
   Development Center
University of Wisconsin
432 North Lake Street,
Rm. 423
Madison, WI 53706
(608) 263-7794
   Eau Claire
   Green Bay
   Kenosha
   La Crosse
   Madison
   Milwaukee
   Oshkosh
   Stevens Points
   Superior
   Whitewater

Wyoming
State Director
WSBDC/State Network Office
111 W. 2nd St., Suite 416
Casper, WY 82601
(307) 235-4825
Casper
  Cheyenne
  Douglas
  Gillette
  Lander
  Laramie
  Powell
  Rock Springs
  Sheridan
  Uinta/Lincoln Counties

Appendix E

Calculating Discounted Cash Flow

In buying a company, you are really interested in the future income stream from the business. That is one - and probably the best - way to assess the value of a company to you as the future owner.

Financial people talk about *discounted cash flow* or *net present value of future payments.* The essence of the idea is that money paid at some time in the future is worth less than money paid today. The reason is that you could be earning interest or dividends or getting appreciation if that money were invested. Since you don't have it, you are losing some of it.

In calculating discounted cash flow, there are two major factors: the discount rate and the time frame. The discount rate is what you think you could have earned on the money. The time frame is how long the payout will go on. The higher the discount rate and the longer the time period, the less the money is worth to you. (There is a section at the end of this report showing how net present value can be calculated.)

Take a simple example. Suppose someone offered to pay you $1,000 in one year. You would get a check for $1,000 at the end of the twelve months. However, had you received the money today, you could have invested it. Suppose you could have earned 10% interest. At the end of the year, you would have $1,100, not $1,000. So you "lost" $100 by waiting to get the money a year later. So the $1,000 paid in a year is worth something less than $1,000. How much? About $909. The reason is that $909 would have earned $91 in interest over the year, and $909 + $91 = $1,000. The net present value of $1,000 in one year at a 10% discount factor is $909.

So if a business generates $100,000 after a year, the deal is actually only worth $90,900.

Sample Calculation of Net Present Value of an Income Stream

Suppose you were interested in purchasing a business that would throw off cash flow as follows:

Year 1	$78,000
Year 2	85,000
Year 3	98,000
Year 4	107,000
Year 5	110,000
Total	478,000

You are being asked to pay $370,000 for the business. On the surface, this looks like a good deal. You pay $370,000 and receive, over five years, $478,000 for a net gain of $108,000.

In looking over the business, you believe it is not terribly risky. Looking through some financial manuals, you find out that the stock market has produced annual returns of 10-11% over periods of ten years or more. So what would happen if you invested your $370,000 in some good mutual funds for five years? Using a basic business calculator, we find that at 10% compounded over five years, the $370,000 would be worth $595,888! So the return from the business doesn't look all that good.

Now let's calculate the net present value of the income stream shown above. We'll use a discount rate of 10%. Here are the results:

Year 1	$78,000	$70,909
Year 2	85,000	70,248
Year 3	98,000	73,629
Year 4	107,000	73,082
Year 5	110,000	68,301
Total	$478,000	$356,169

The apparent $478,000 is actually worth only $356,169 which is less than the purchase price of $370,000.

A discount rate of 10% may be too low for this example. The reason is that this single small business is riskier than a mutual fund where the risk is spread of many businesses perhaps in a variety of different kinds of commerce. Let's use a discount rate of 15%.

Year 1	$78,000	$68,826
Year 2	85,000	64,272
Year 3	98,000	64,437
Year 4	107,000	61,178

| Year 5 | 110,000 | 54,689 |
| Total | $478,000 | $313,402 |

You can see that the higher discount rate results in a lower total pay out estimate.

Calculating net present value is relatively simple on a calculator or spread sheet. You enter the *amount of money* (in dollars) to be paid at some future date, the *number of years (n)* until that happens, and the *discount rate* (%). The calculator or spread sheet computes the present value.

INDEX

Order Form

Send orders to:
Chief Mountain Publishing
4346 West Pondview Drive
Littleton, Colorado 80123.

Checks or money orders only please. No C.O.D.

$15.95 + $3.00 shipping and handling. Colorado residents please add 3% sales tax. Allow two weeks for delivery. If multiple copies are ordered, please add $1.00 shipping and handling for each additional book.

Please send _____ additional copies of ***Make $$$ Buying and Selling Small Businesses.***

Send to:

Name: _____

Address_____

City: _____State:_____

Zip:_____Phone: ( )_____